Springer Series in Supply Chain Management

Volume 16

Supply Chain Management (SCM), long an integral part of Operations Management, focuses on all elements of creating a product or service, and delivering that product or service, at the optimal cost and within an optimal timeframe. It spans the movement and storage of raw materials, work-in-process inventory, and finished goods from point of origin to point of consumption. To facilitate physical flows in a time-efficient and cost-effective manner, the scope of SCM includes technology-enabled information flows and financial flows.

The Springer Series in Supply Chain Management, under the guidance of founding Series Editor Christopher S. Tang, covers research of either theoretical or empirical nature, in both authored and edited volumes from leading scholars and practitioners in the field – with a specific focus on topics within the scope of SCM.

This series has been accepted by Scopus.

Springer and the Series Editor welcome book ideas from authors. Potential authors who wish to submit a book proposal should contact Ms. Jialin Yan, Associate Editor, Springer (Germany), e-mail: jialin.yan@springernature.com

Sanchay Roy • Stewart Dunbar

Improving Supply Chains in the Oil and Gas Industry

12 Modules to Improve Chronic Challenges for Maintenance, Repair and Operations

Foreword by Knut Alicke

Springer

Sanchay Roy
The Hague, The Netherlands

Stewart Dunbar
Flitch Green, Essex, UK

ISSN 2365-6395 ISSN 2365-6409 (electronic)
Springer Series in Supply Chain Management
ISBN 978-3-030-95065-1 ISBN 978-3-030-95066-8 (eBook)
https://doi.org/10.1007/978-3-030-95066-8

This Springer imprint is published by the registered company Springer Nature Switzerland AG
The registered company address is: Gewerbestrasse 11, 6330 Cham, Switzerland

"It is not the strongest of the species that survives; nor the most intelligent that survives. It is the one most adaptable to change."

.. its been said before.

Dedication

To our parents, our lovely wives,
two daughters, a son and a dog.

In the memory of my Father. I wish we had more time together.

Foreword

For the last 25 years, I have been helping companies across all sectors to improve their supply chain performance and prepare for the future. Topics range from setting up integrated planning processes, ensuring the right organisational structure, governance and incentives, optimising the physical distribution network, manufacturing and sourcing through to ways of predicting the future with new algorithms like machine learning. I am passionate about building/improving the capabilities of supply chain professionals and adjacent functions as an important enabler of sustainable change.

This is where my journey with Sanchay started. Attending the McKinsey Supply Chain Executive Academy, Sanchay and I started a very fruitful journey of brainstorming and continuous exchange on the latest and greatest ideas across the supply chain. Sanchay gave a tremendous keynote on supply chain management in oil and gas in one of the later sessions of this event. He also contributed to a book I wrote (*Supply Chain Segmentation*, Springer Publications) in 2015 with a chapter on Philips Case Study and has always been eager to improve and give back to the supply chain community.

In 2019, Sanchay and Stewart approached me with the idea of writing a book on how to improve the supply chain in oil and gas. I was extremely supportive for this important topic, to review, brainstorm and write a foreword—and indeed, here we are.

Supply chain is a relatively young discipline—having its roots in fast-moving consumer goods (FMCG) and consumer electronics it developed into an important pillar for success for many other industries. It covers end-to-end planning, involving sales, manufacturing, procurement and finance in a regular process facilitated by supply chain managers to prepare for the order intake, to ensure the right availability of products and finally to deliver to the customer what they ordered on time. The latest developments in digital have helped create a depth of visibility in the end-to-end process from customers to suppliers to further improve the supply chain performance. With the advent of e-commerce, the customer experience in placing an order, having an instant view on availability and ultimately a reliable delivery is appreciated by all of us and in turn has also led to a change in business-to-business transactions. On the journey, the supply chain manager evolved from someone who was only visible if something went wrong to a critical enabler of success—this is reflected by the many chief supply chain officers we see in today's organisations.

But hold on—do all these concepts and processes make sense in the oil and gas supply chain? In my daily work I often hear questions like integrated planning and visibility are nice in other industries, but are they really applicable in oil and gas? Is not the focus different?

Not at all—these principles still apply and help a lot in oil and gas as Sanchay and Stewart lay out in this excellent book.

The oil and gas industry has, and will continue, to focus on production—topics like the supply chain maintenance, repair, and operations (MRO) are important, but traditionally approached on a 'just in case' basis. Hugh piles of inventory make managers feel secure against any stoppages which would result in huge and immediate losses in revenue. Time is of the essence and spare parts/equipment availability is key—the cost of losing an hour of production is very high and delayed projects can be even higher! At the same time spares need to be planned very carefully; it does not help if a part has gone beyond its shelf life or simply cannot be found in the enormous mountains of inventory.

Sanchay and Stewart experienced these shortcomings and took action—they improved the supply chains they were responsible for applying concepts they learned in other industries and discovered a huge and untapped improvement potential. It is great to see how they brought advanced supply chain management concepts to the oil and gas industry to change the way MRO is operated. The outbreak of the COVID-19 pandemic also accelerated the need for a well-functioning/well-oiled MRO machine.

Sanchay and Stewart have developed a holistic framework consisting of 12 elements to configure, plan and execute the MRO supply chain. Sustainable impact is only achieved through a holistic approach, complementing the technical part with a change in mindset and the right capabilities to work together in the end-to-end supply chain.

I like the wealth of practical advice like *'Fail to plan? Then plan to fail'*, redefining the well-known sales and operations planning (S&OP) process into a 'planning and operations planning (P&OP)' planning and many other tips and tricks. The concepts introduced are deeply rooted in practical supply chain applied in the oil and gas sector.

The lead time from idea to book was extremely short. Sanchay and Stewart did a great job not only describing supply chain, but even developing a practical framework and focusing on technical, capability and change topics.

The book should serve as a playbook to improve supply chain in oil and gas. Thank you Sanchay and Stewart for bringing it to life. Enjoy reading the book.

McKinsey & Company,
Berlin, Germany

University of Cologne,
Cologne, Germany

Knut Alicke

Karlsruhe, Germany
November 2021

About the Authors

The idea for this book arose after the global outbreak of COVID-19 in March 2019. This was soon followed by the low oil price which witnessed one of the global oil indices drop into a negative position for the first time in history. The oil majors declined to make dividend payments for the first time since the Second World War, and there was a question mark over the future of these behemoths.

We were part of a task force to understand the vulnerability in the upstream inbound supply chain, where it gave us an unusual opportunity to look 'under the bonnet' of this organisation and consider impacts and consequences of things outside of our day-to-day tasks.

We do not profess to be experts in all of the areas we have discussed in this book, but we have had the opportunity to piece together the common threads and the limitations imposed. In some cases, COVID-19 had a detrimental impact, but in others it forced a change in the organisation that under normal circumstances would never have been considered.

We wrote this book late in the evenings and weekends, across continents from Nigeria to the Netherlands to the UK, with the blessing (sometimes we suspect reluctantly) from our families as an opportunity to share what we saw and encourage a discussion to happen on a broader scale across other IOCs and like-minded peer groups.

We are at the start of this journey; we have by no means solved the problem nor do we profess to have all the best solutions, but we have attempted to define the problems and suggest ways they can be tackled from our own experiences and observations.

Thank you for reading our book, and we wish you well in your personal journeys.

Sanchay Roy is a seasoned professional with a great deal of experience in supply chain and Lean methodology. He has worked across several sectors including oil and gas, consumer goods and chemicals. He is a global operation, supply chain and continuous improvement professional with a broad background in business transformations.

As a global professional, he has lived and worked in India, the UK, Germany, Belgium and the Netherlands and has had significant work experience in China,

Southeast Asia and East Europe. He has managed global programmes in supply chain, Lean Six Sigma, quality, e-business and industrial design.

In his current role Sanchay has been transforming the maintenance, repair and operations supply chains. This transformation is across plan-source-make-deliver value streams and includes deployment of digital tools to create supply chain control towers. Prior to his current role, Sanchay was responsible for deploying a fit-for-purpose, effective continuous improvement strategy that greatly streamlined capital projects' execution and significantly improved productivity and performance.

Before joining Shell, Sanchay ran global Operations and Supply Chain for the Consumer Luminaires division of Philips Lighting, receiving the CEO Award for the Best Run Supply Chain Function. He also led the Business Transformation for Philips Lighting and deployed Lean manufacturing and continuous improvement across +50 manufacturing sites globally. Sanchay started his career with GE, where he held many business and leadership roles and earned his Master Black Belt and a Lean Master accreditation.

Sanchay is an industrial design graduate from the National Institute of Design, India. He lives in Den Haag, Netherlands, with his wife and two daughters. He enjoys motorcycling, ultralight flying and reading.

Stewart Dunbar has a learner mindset. He has worked in various supply chains for over 30 years, in industries ranging from the upstream energy sector to FMCG. In addition to this, he has been a supply chain consultant developing and executing strategies as well as operational improvements using Lean principles.

Stewart currently works as the materials management manager and is responsible for all MRO material movement and storage for Shell Nigeria, which generates revenues worth ~$3 billion.

Prior to this role, he was instrumental in driving performance improvements in the downstream lubricants supply chain through the consolidation and reduction of production plants. He started his career working in distribution within Tesco Stores Limited in the UK and moved on to hold positions ranging from planning and performance manager through to managing a UK distribution centre, supply chain strategy development and supply chain management where he was responsible for the procurement of adult drinks with annual sales in excess of $2.3 billion. He then moved to Sainsburys to help drive operational improvements in their legacy sites as they moved through their automation programme. Finally, he was a consultant for over 5 years in the UK, working with the Co-Op, Arla Foods, Frontline Publishing and DHL.

Stewart gained his degree in mathematics from Brunel University and has an inquisitive mind for numbers. He lives in Essex, UK, with his wife and son. He is an avid reader and also enjoys motorcycling and travelling.

Acknowledgements

Our journey began in 2019 during a team session in Nigeria. We had just spent three days with some of the most dedicated and knowledgeable experts from procurement, maintenance, operations and category leads with years of experience in the industry. We argued, blamed each other and felt really frustrated about the state of affairs, but in the end, we realised that the 'supply chain' was not operating as it should. Those that needed equipment and material could not see how they influenced the demand at the start of the chain preferring to focus on the lack of material availability, the procurement team observed that anything but cost was important, and the value stream execution teams did not understand that they could influence the demand to make life better. Our heartfelt thanks to Scott Low and Roberta Oshiobugie for pulling us right in the middle of a core business vulnerability. Over the next 18 months as we visited many assets and joint ventures run by international and national oil companies, we started to see a common pattern emerge despite the differences in countries, locations and complexity of operations. These observations and our personal experiences formed the basis for this book.

In 2020, when the pandemic started, the organisations quickly realised that the supply chain was indeed a critical cog in the machinery and that, despite robust business continuity plans in place, this global event was beyond what had ever been considered. At this stage, we were tasked with identifying how to better understand the vulnerabilities that existed in our value stream so that they could be tackled. We would like to thank both Jack Heng and the team from McKinsey for working with us to design, develop and deploy a framework based on supply chain fundamentals that could be applied across all assets.

18 months later, the importance of the supply chain has remained the centre of attention for most businesses and the global economy. We have seen little signs of this situation abating, and the way businesses deal with it will ultimately determine their future.

The idea for this book first appeared just after this exercise as we quickly concluded that the supply chain in the oil and gas industry is precariously balanced and heavily weighted towards the discipline of engineering rather than supply chain expertise. We enriched the concept with conversations with frontline teams. They shared their stories and experiences that helped us deepen our understanding and join the dots between diverse factors and functions.

This book is about capturing our experience and insights from our dialogues. We studied the history of the business and are observing the sociopolitical forces that are driving the current transformations. We connected with leaders and frontline operators who are lifers in the business, with little external perspective outside of the O&G sector. We also connected with our network of supply chain professionals in other industries to make a comparative understanding of the gaps. This book is based on those conversations. This is not a technical book.

Our heartfelt thanks to Knut Alicke, Partner at McKinsey, for his review and deep insights into MRO supply chains. Special thanks to Patrick Rowe, Supply Chain Consultant, for the detailed review and improvement suggestions. Jialin Yan of Springer Publications for encouragement and motivation. Those who have employed us and allowed us to develop our supply chain appreciation and many colleagues at our workplace who have challenged and developed our insights.

Last but not the least, Ruchita, Carol and our children for their patience and giving up the weekends and evenings for this book. We would not have managed this without you holding the fort. Thank you all!

A Note to the Reader

Supply chains are designed to streamline the flow of goods and information. A good supply chain will be resilient to uncertainties and prepare itself in advance. Keeping that in mind, you, the reader, can read the chapters in the book as we intended them to be or may decide that you just cannot wait and jump straight to the twelve modules of transformation (Chap. 5). You can always decide to come back to earlier chapters to reflect on whether the origins of supply chain challenges in your organisation bear any resemblance to the ones we discuss here or are completely different. As much as we look forward with the aim of improvement, it is always good to reflect on the past and capture all the lessons learned and experience gathered. It is said that hindsight is 20:20, but these experiences can and should be used to create clarity for the future. Either way, once you have been through the chapters, we hope that you have sufficient insights for your journey of transformation. The energy industry is at a crossroads, and it is transforming. Whether it is transforming quickly enough, time will judge but supply chains are at the very core and are central to a successful transition.

To understand better the nature of the supply chain being described in this book, it is essential that we briefly explore the difference between a traditional view of a supply chain and a maintenance, repair and operations (MRO) supply chain. The traditional definition of a supply chain is a sequence of processes involved in the production and distribution of a commodity to a consumer. An MRO supply chain on the other hand is one which ensures the serviceability of a production unit or the delivery of a construction project, where there is no final consumer. The MRO supply chain ensures the continuance or development of a company enabling a revenue source, rather than delivering the revenue itself.

Additionally, elements of the same supply chain will be considered differently depending on whose perspective is being used. Say for example a company such as GE which provides materials to an oil and gas company will regard this supply chain as a traditional one since there is a commodity produced and a customer at the end of it. However, from the perspective of the oil and gas company, this is an MRO supply chain, which is supporting operations and development to facilitate production.

This book has been created from the observations made of the MRO supply chains across the industry.

Contents

Chapter 1
Lower Forever

1.1 Sacred Sectors

When I was growing up, there were always two businesses that were considered to be as 'safe as houses', the banks and the oil companies. The comments used to be that 'Joe has a great job in banking, they will do well, the banks are a really safe place to work'. And so, it was with the oil industry—this person has been out on the rigs or working in Saudi, we will always need oil. That was what they said...

Then in 2008 along came the global financial crisis which blew a hole in the notion that banks were as safe as the houses they offered mortgages on, the financial world rocked on its axis and needed to reassess their lot in life, to re-address the way they operated, the way they sat behind their corporate desks feeling invincible.

Dr. Philip Verleger, who has studied and written about energy markets since 1971 (www.pkverlegerllc.com), observed that to 2019 there had been 19 historical oil disruptions in the last 40 years, and he forecasted that the 20th would shock the markets. In 2020, his predictions came true and although he did not forecast COVID-19, oil supply outstripped the demand in a market where people were quarantined, where the daily commute ceased, and the oil industry was well and truly out of sorts. On 20th April 2020, the West Texas Intermediate oil price collapsed to below (negative) \$30, customers needed to be paid to take the oil away! There was no storage capacity and no demand, and the oil prices crashed around the world.

But what is so different about the recovery from this crash and the other 19, surely the market will just bounce back? No doubt we will see the return to the consumption levels seen previously, we always have in the past.

Similar to the banking situation, the notion that an ever-expanding market with a level of growth capable of sustaining investment to drive even more growth was wrong. This 20th crash was the one that signalled a change in mindset, customers questioned the need for consumption of oil, businesses wondered (and are still wondering) whether to retain their office buildings and people are continuing to

S. Roy, S. Dunbar, *Improving Supply Chains in the Oil and Gas Industry*, Springer Series in Supply Chain Management 16,
https://doi.org/10.1007/978-3-030-95066-8_1

work from home reducing the need for commuting. Families are questioning whether they need multiple cars they once thought they did and whether they should be going green anyway. What we see is a low oil price that is likely to be around for a long time.

The oil companies have learnt from previous market crashes, haven't they? After 19 major crashes, you would think so, but maybe not, if the good times are always believed to be round the corner, superficial adjustment and window dressing were sufficient to make the problem survivable, and because the market would return, the same type (if not always the same level) of resource would be needed.

In 2020, the energy sector was rocked on its axis, as the banking sector was in 2008. This crash has left industry with surplus capacity and bloated costs. To effect a change, the industry needs to overhaul its strategy, re-align the direction and embrace new energies. There is also an ever-increasing sociopolitical pressure to reduce the overall carbon footprint. The energy sector must jettison its old habits and the waste it has allowed to grow over the last 50 years.

1.2 Call Me Back in 30 mins

I was an experienced hire in a major International Oil Company. Coming from the consumer industries where the mantra of lean was more than two decades old, I came in confident with the notion that applying time-tested lean methodologies would be a fantastic opportunity for operational excellence and cost saving. Then I encountered the narrow-minded attitude that has led to the growth in waste of inventory. I recount one particular incident very clearly. One of the new graduates found an opportunity to save \$150 k in pipeline inventory by the creation of more accurate Bills of Materials. Eager to share his idea he called up his asset manager to share the opportunity. The asset manager listened to him and then asked the graduate to call him back in 30 min. The graduate attributed this to a busy schedule but an active interest of the asset manager. So, after 30 min, he called up the asset manager and eagerly asked what he thought about the improvement and the replication opportunities.

The asset manager then told him that in the last 30 min while the graduate waited, he had pulled out more dollars from the seabed than his measly inventory improvement opportunity. He then proceeded to admonish him by telling him never to call again regarding inventory improvement opportunities. With the cash he was pulling out of the ground, he could have fields of the pipelines and not worry about them.

And literally, fields of inventory of all sorts of pipelines, equipment, spare parts ranging from 5 to 25 years old is commonplace in most Oil and Gas assets. In some assets, 25–28 warehouses are filled with parts and equipment worth hundreds of millions. Many of them bought as expensive 'insurance spares' lie around for decades and are poorly preserved. Naturally, when the asset actually needs them, the equipment may be too old or unreliable to risk being used in operations. Thus, a new part is ordered all over again at a huge expense. Interestingly no one is truly accountable for this working capital, since production and the availability of an asset is a top priority, operations and maintenance would rather simply order a new part or piece of equipment. To add to this, if the lead time for delivery is too long then they will often just order an extra one as 'insurance' or the entire piece of equipment itself, so that parts can be scavenged from it when needed. These items bought directly from the suppliers would go into operations or maintenance inventory stores, often called 'squirrel stores' and we all know what squirrel stores contain!

These squirrel stores are full of unaccounted and uncontrolled inventory worth multiple billions of dollars, having grown through the heydays of oil price when profits achieved easily drowned any such inefficiency, unimaginable in most other industries.

The issue does not just end here. One would ask, surely, we can do a clean-up, get rid of old inventory, and return the working capital back to manageable levels. However, aged inventory loses its physical dimensions and simply becomes a number on a financial spreadsheet—a true no-man's land. Once there, the inventory can hold its original value in digital form for decades, even if the physical part has rusted away to a piece of useless metal in the elements. These cannot be sold as they still hold the original value in the books but the second-hand market will not pay these prices. No asset manager worth his/her annual performance bonus will ever take the hit on cost performance by writing off millions from the plants and equipment, worse still if one must pay to dispose of the materials. Thus, most asset leaders would rather 'live-with' or ignore the topic until they change jobs, and it becomes someone else's problem. The material lives on as their digital avatar in finance books while the actual inventory is long forgotten in a squirrel store of a 'loving and careful' operations or maintenance manager.

1.3 Change Is Nigh

This once titan of industries is being rocked at its core. The popularity and desire for oil and gas have waned significantly across the globe for a multitude of reasons.

The desire to move away from hydrocarbon usage and into cleaner energy of the future has taken away the option of the oil companies to simply 'ride out the storm', it has changed the way the first world looks at its carbon production.

The central pillar of the 2015 Paris Agreement committed to keeping a global temperature rise this century well below 2 °C above pre-industrial levels and to pursue efforts to limit the temperature increase even further to 1.5 degrees. In contrast to this, oil companies rushed to acquire oil and gas fields and bring the crude or natural gas to market. Now, analysts say, investors are sceptical of all but the most profitable investments in fossil fuels because it is not clear that there will be future demand for them.

Ensuing price wars (an often-used tool for political gains) between OPEC, Russia, and the USA have further put downward pressures on the value of oil and gas. In addition, the COVID threat continues to add sustained pressure as a result of ongoing discoveries of new variants. Figure 1.1 shows the volatility of oil price to significant events. Top all this off with the impact of COVID-19 means that there is no confidence that a full bounceback of the oil prices will happen and has the majors writing down the value of their oil and gas assets (Fig. 1.2).

Less than a decade ago, Exxon Mobil was the most valuable company in the world. Recently, it was removed from Dow Jones industrial average after nearly a century of inclusion in the stock index. Most people did not predict that demand for fossil fuels would start to wane, until it did. Today, all of Exxon is worth less than Jeff Bezos, personal net worth. The sacred sectors are losing their place in the world.

This external shift in the market has created a complex situation for the Oil and Gas industry, the dichotomy between continuing to produce in what would be a shrinking market or transferring their focus into the new energy sector, where carbon neutrality is the target. Even up until 2019, the sector still anticipated significant growth by 2030 (Fig. 1.3).

Well, here is the dilemma, continue with your head in the sand pretending nothing has changed or effectively gamble on a much smaller less developed market. In reality, the Oil and Gas players have decided to take a hybrid approach to resolve this issue—maximise the value from the old energy to fund development in the new energy sector. In 2021, Shell announced that it internally would be carbon neutral by 2035 and that by 2050 this would be extended to its suppliers as well.

Ultimately this may turn out to be the transition era where oil giants, especially in Europe, started looking more like electric companies.

In 2020, Royal Dutch Shell won a deal to build a vast wind farm off the coast of the Netherlands. Earlier in the year, France's Total, which owns a battery maker, agreed to make several large investments in solar power in Spain and a wind farm off Scotland. Total also bought an electric and natural gas utility in Spain and is joining Shell and BP in expanding its electric vehicle charging business.

At the same time, the companies are ditching plans to drill more wells as they chop back capital budgets. Shell recently said it would delay new fields in the Gulf of Mexico and in the North Sea, while BP has promised not to explore for oil in any new countries.

Prodded by governments and investors to address climate change concerns about their products, Europe's oil companies are accelerating their production of cleaner energy—usually electricity, sometimes hydrogen—and promoting natural gas, which they argue can be a cleaner transition fuel from coal and oil to renewables.

For some executives, the sudden plunge in demand for oil caused by the pandemic—and the accompanying collapse in earnings—is another warning that unless they change the composition of their businesses, they risk walking the same path as dinosaurs did, straight into extinction.

This evolving vision is more striking because it is shared by many long-time veterans of the oil business.

All of Europe's large oil companies have now set targets to reduce the carbon emissions that contribute to climate change. Most have set a 'net zero' ambition by

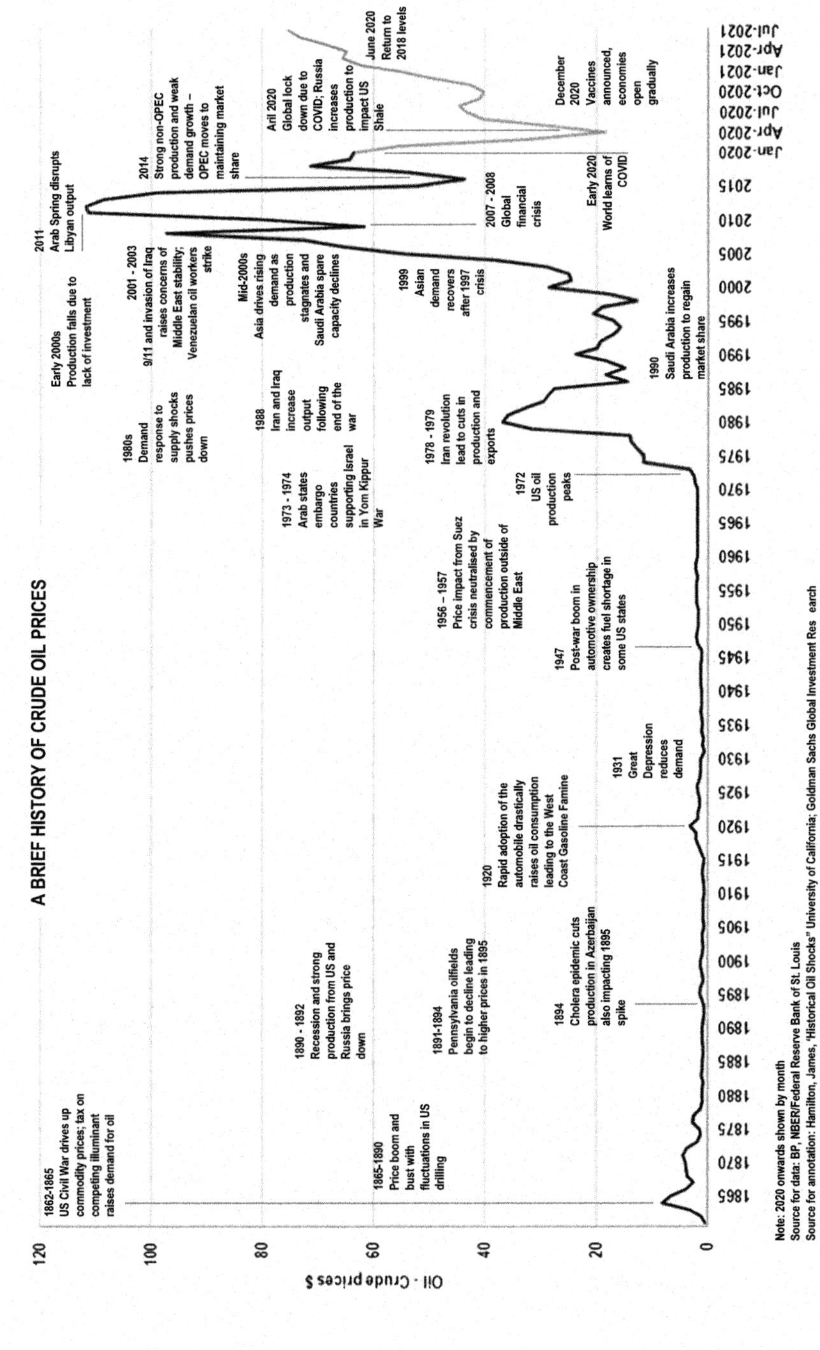

Fig. 1.1 The oil price and global events

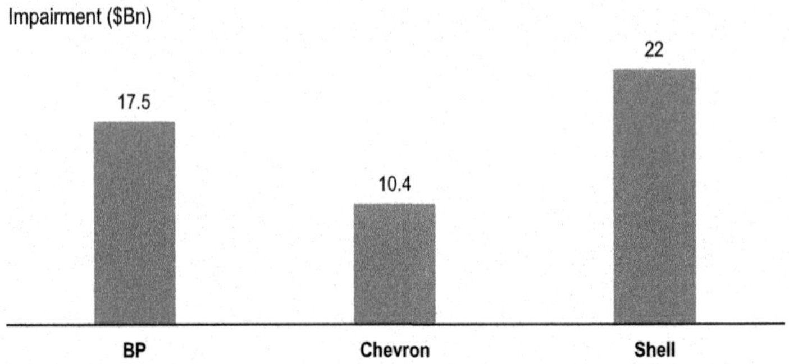

Fig. 1.2 The impairments announced

2050, a goal also embraced by governments like the European Union and the United Kingdom.

The companies plan to get there by selling more and more renewable energy and, in some cases, by offsetting emissions with so-called nature-based solutions like planting forests to soak up carbon. While there is scepticism in both the environmental and the investment communities about whether century-old companies like BP and Shell can learn new tricks, they do bring scale and know-how to the task.

'To make a switch from a global economy that depends on fossil fuels for 80 percent of its energy to something else is a very, very big job,' said Daniel

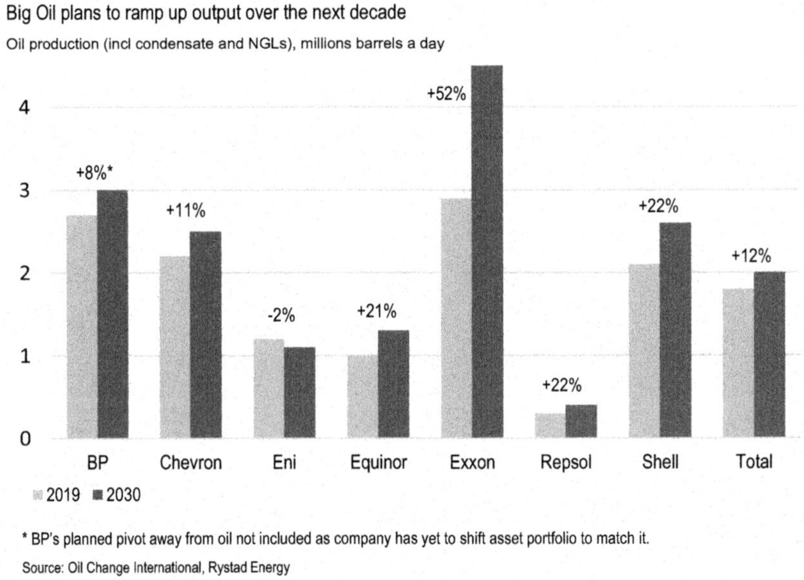

Fig. 1.3 External pressure and internal response

Yergin, the energy historian who has a forthcoming book, 'The New Map', on the transition now occurring in energy. But he noted, 'These companies are really good at big, complex engineering management that will be required for a transition of that scale'.

Financial analysts say the dreadnoughts are already changing course. 'They are doing it because management believes it is the right thing to do and also because shareholders are severely pressuring them', said Michele Della Vigna, head of natural resources research at Goldman Sachs.

The Oil Majors have a big hill to climb with this transition, to generate enough cash in a depressed market, with a declining popularity, to fund the creation of an equally strong and resilient company in the new energy sector. The first port of call for the Oil and Gas Companies has been to focus their efforts on those projects and assets that generate great benefits and away from the more marginal ones, to ditch the risky parts of the business and let low cost and indigenous operators take them on.

However, the real question is whether this is enough? If the low and marginal profit-making assets are disposed of, what is left is a business that still needs to maximise its earnings to ensure accelerated investment into the new energies. The stability of the oil price is anything but assured, therefore it is critical that every last cent is saved by focusing attention on optimising cost as well as ensuring good production levels whilst at the same time reducing inventory. Now is the time to divert all attention on resolving the issues across the supply chain and truly reap the benefits to be found here.

Chapter 2
The OPEX Challenge

2.1 When the Going Gets Tough…

Winston Churchill is credited with the statement 'Never let a good crisis go to waste' when he was working to form the United Nations after WW2. This was a time when the world had indeed made a significant detrimental impact on itself, ravaging nations, leaving industry on the floor and driving its population to the edge of despair. There could only be one way and that was up.

The low oil price and COVID-19 impact are by comparison on a different scale, but the sentiment remains the same. The internal focus within oil companies has quickly turned to operating expenses (OPEX).

Back in 2016, Accenture published a paper on Five Essentials for Improving Operating Costs (in the energy sector). In it, they talk about the need for Oil and Gas companies to 'abandon traditional cost-cutting responses to adverse market conditions and work collaboratively with suppliers to manage costs and protect margins'. They highlight the link between short-term cost-cutting and value erosion, a win–lose (or lose–win) situation.

Accenture advises that a much better solution is to focus on five essential activities to manage costs effectively and to deliver sustainable business improvements:

- Think margin, not just production.
- Scrutinize costs and focus on controlling their drivers.
- Concentrate on improving baseline production.
- Share risks and rewards with suppliers.
- Change culture: place greater emphasis on planning, accountability and service quality.

The Oil and Gas majors are looking hard in some of these areas. The natural and easy one to focus on is number 3—concentrating on baseline production, since this is

S. Roy, S. Dunbar, *Improving Supply Chains in the Oil and Gas Industry*, Springer Series in Supply Chain Management 16,
https://doi.org/10.1007/978-3-030-95066-8_2

(and always has been) the go-to place for the technical guys. Some inroads have been made into looking at margins (number 1), with Shell and Total being very selective about the projects to be jettisoned based on the likely benefit to be gained. In fact, Shell has recently announced that beyond 2025 there will be no further frontier upstream exploration. Both BP and Shell have declared they want to be carbon neutral by 2050, which will no doubt mean reduced production levels, driving them to put a much greater focus on profitable production rather than production at any cost. This will in turn go towards funding the investment into cleaner and greener energies which is a good step forward. These approaches align with Accenture's first step but again the question is: will it be enough?

With reference to the second essential activity, scrutinising costs, the 'slash it now and protect today' approach is a habit the energy sector finds hard to kick and it is a reflex reaction. The easiest approach is to reduce manpower, to focus on lowering costs and to cancel many projects regardless of who gets hurt in the process. This approach will and does reduce the cost in the short term but is unsustainable and the very fact that it is still the 'go-to' solution means that the leaders of these businesses are reverting to type. The oil giants are waking up to this, with BP announcing in 2020, 10,000 job cuts and Shell announcing up to 9000 a few weeks later.

The industry leans very heavily on getting the best 'value' (read lowest cost) from the vendors, so the fourth step (share risks and rewards with suppliers) is truly uncharted water, unlike automotive and aerospace industries where tiers 2 and 3 are deeply integrated into the overall design, development and delivery. Only recently have the oil and gas projects begun to adopt a standardised off the shelf approach to project design driven by time and cost pressures at the Front-End Engineering Design stage. From a risk perspective, the Oil and Gas sector has been much more liberal and successful in sharing their safety framework with their suppliers. However, will these behemoths recognise that by sharing knowledge, risks and rewards drives a fundamental change in the end-to-end processes that would enable both the oil companies and their suppliers to benefit, a better solution should be the aim rather than lower costs.

The largest gap in the current strategies within the industry is Accenture's fifth essential activity—Change culture: place greater emphasis on planning, accountability and service quality. This element is the one significant omission across their plans. By its omission, their ability to achieve a credible and sustainable reduction in costs (the second essential) is severely limited.

This gap is apparent in the industry due to the size and complexity of these companies. One area may well have adopted a very strong approach to changing the culture, but this is rare and isolated across the business. Therefore, even where it is adopted, it is very fragile due to the regular turnover of leadership. This fragility leads to significant culture changes following a change in leader, if the culture were indeed embedded properly the new leader's attention would be to continuously improve performance rather than reinvent the team's approach. The thoughts and ideas following in the section dealing with the 12 modules address this specific area.

2.2 Production at any Price?

In other industries, when the demand reduces, strategic decisions are made to either reduce production or to stockpile for the future. Either way, the individual organisations are free to make these decisions on their own. In the Oil and Gas industry, this freedom is largely absent as it requires alignment between a number of different organisations, all with different priorities and agendas. Balancing production based on market dynamics is a significant challenge.

There are three differentiators that have a major impact on the way this sector is able to respond to the market dynamics:

- Ownership: Oftentimes the most significant stakeholder in these ventures is the government who relies on this income as a fundamental pillar of the economy to survive. In the case of Nigeria, oil and gas revenues generated more than 80% of foreign exchange revenues, in Russia this is around 50%, therefore critical to both their national economies and for their governments in power.
- Governance: Globally there are three behemoths in the production of Oil and Gas: Russia, 13 members of OPEC and the USA with its shale production. The origins and ideologies of these bodies do not align and probably never will. Therefore, the control of global prices is a very sensitive issue and can destabilize individual nations. The moves in 2020 which lead to the negative value of the WTI for the first time in history indicate that the existing production governance is not sufficiently reactive to sharp changes in demand.
- Shareholder: Primary motivation for an oil and gas company is to deliver what is known as free cash flow (FCF). FCF is earnings net of taxes minus CAPEX, which delivers the ability to pay dividends. In order to remain a target investment for the financial markets, dividends must be maintained. Recent actions of removing dividends have hurt this industry significantly and are likely to suppress the market valuation for a prolonged period of time.

Because there are larger forces at play it is critical that the focus is given to minimising OPEX and generating FCF regardless of global oil prices. As discussed earlier, impacts from COVID, society and the desire to transition to a carbon neutral business will keep the pressure on this industry for the foreseeable future. A reliable supply chain for maintenance, repair and operations (MRO) is a key dimension for optimising OPEX.

Chapter 3
Supply Chain Development in Oil and Gas Industry

3.1 How We Got to Where We Are?

The oil and gas sector is a very specialised and focused industry, where deep knowledge and experience is the norm. Often there is a significant level of government involvement through either shared ownership and/or strict regulatory controls. Making genuine mistakes in some countries can lead to arrest and imprisonment. On the other hand, due to the level of government involvement and the size of contract awards, there can often be an unhealthy tension between trying to achieve the best outcome and satisfying senior partner expectations.

Because of its specialism and the deep knowledge required it drives a very close-knit community that is often too internally focused and seldom looks outside for either benchmarking or inspiration, to the extent that the recognised benchmarking companies focus solely on the Oil and Gas sector. Even in functions that are common across businesses such as contracting, supply chain, HR, vendor performance management, there is little benchmarking outside of Oil and Gas. This intra-sector navel gazing results in top quartile industry performance levels that are significantly below the level that could be achieved.

Looking into the O&G companies, this deep knowledge has driven specialisms such as supply chain to be created simply as though they are a necessary evil to support the primary goal of the engineering and production aspirations of the company. In addition to this, there is a mistaken belief that only those who have worked in the production or engineering side understand how the business operates and therefore are appointed into supply chain roles for which they have little or no qualification or relevant experience. This has created an entry barrier for external supply chain professionals which is notably prevalent at the ranks of senior leadership. Combine this with the introspective nature of the business, then the same mistakes or suboptimal practices are perpetuated from one generation to the next.

S. Roy, S. Dunbar, *Improving Supply Chains in the Oil and Gas Industry*, Springer Series in Supply Chain Management 16,
https://doi.org/10.1007/978-3-030-95066-8_3

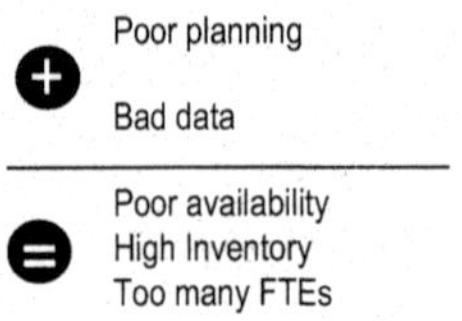

Fig. 3.1 The relationships

From a technology perspective, until recently spreadsheets and the like were the only forms of systems in these critical support functions of the multi-billion dollar companies. Even now new technology is often only at the level that would have been widespread across FMCG during the 1980s and before this in the automotive industry (barcoding, network connectivity, handheld terminals, auto inventory optimisation).

The combined impact of these issues has resulted over the years in vast amounts of waste throughout the organisation, ranging from manual processing and high levels of equipment and spares inventory. The consequence is that not only are the inventory levels excessive, but there is a second level of hidden inventory that has been procured for projects either cancelled or overbought *just in case* due to a lack of trust in the supply chain. Excuses abound including long lead time items, market shortages, buy three to ensure one etc. These excess inventories can add to hundreds of millions of dollars lying around. In one asset alone, containers of surplus stock covered 23 football pitches. It is key to recognise the impact of poor planning and data (Fig. 3.1).

We estimate that between 25 and 30% of unscheduled deferment[1] or lack of production availability is caused by failures created in the end-to-end MRO supply chain. This can seriously impact the interval between incidents (i.e., the frequency of failure increases) as well as extend the mean time taken to complete repairs. Overall, this has two major impacts, in the short term a detrimental effect on production levels but just as importantly a reduction in the longevity of the equipment in service.

By not addressing these fundamental issues, the benefits from deploying technology are oftentimes undermined by poor processes and a lack of end-to-end understanding driving a silo execution mentality. For example, achieving a reduction in spares inventory without considering the impact on the operation is at best foolhardy.

The industry as a whole is much more investment driven therefore much more susceptible to asset stripping. The only true USP in upstream is the innovative engineering solutions, for example deepwater exploration, sour gas management,

[1] "Deferment" in Oil and Gas context is a term where the extraction of oil and gas from a reservoir is delayed as a consequence of a stop in operation. Since the resource is still available in the reservoir, this is not considered a production loss but a production deferment. We believe that since the production of the same barrel of oil at a later date is met with the prevailing market prices, it therefore has an impact on operating profits and thus the concept of deferment as a concept of "delayed" versus "lost" production can be misleading. Figure 3.2 shows how deferment is tracked in addition to production.

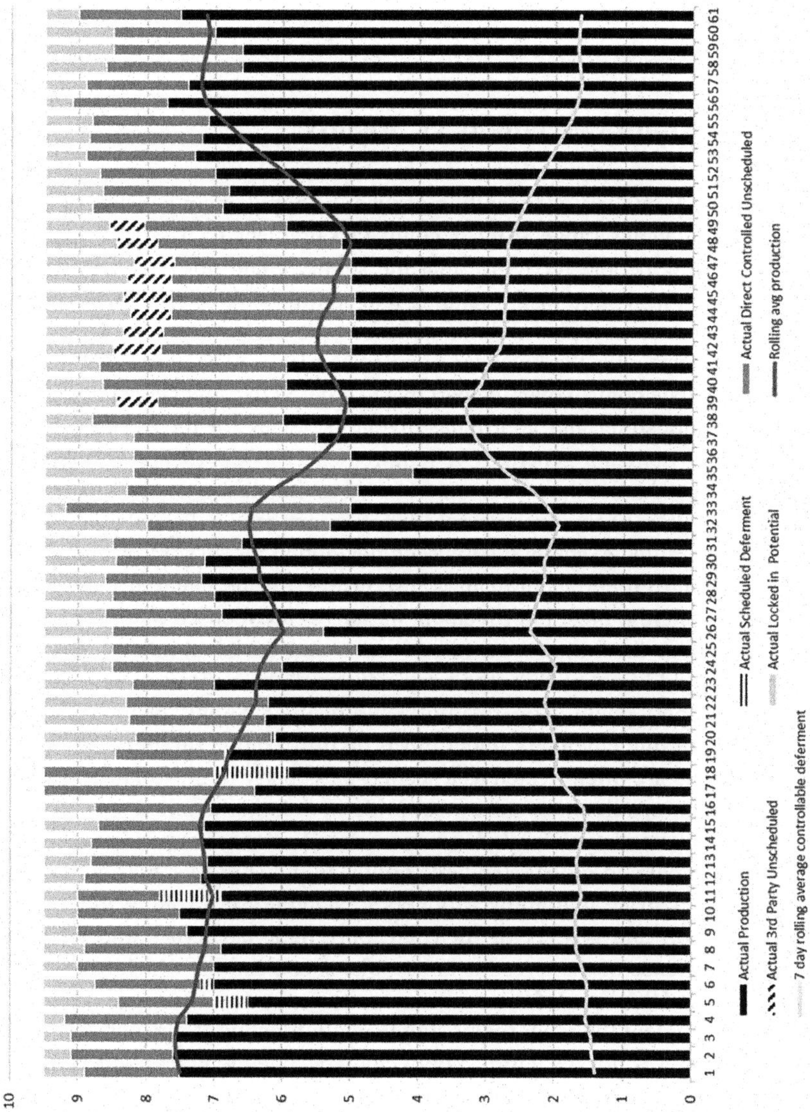

Fig. 3.2 Typical daily production and deferment

horizontal drilling, reservoir management, decommissioning etc. There is a lack of appreciation of the benefits of an integrated supply chain and its impact on the upstream business and its profitability. We are reliant on the commodity market price of oil, when it is good it is great and when it is bad everyone runs around like headless chickens.

3.2 Supply Chain Perception Vs. Reality

There is still a very mixed understanding of what a supply chain consists of within this industry. The views range from it being Procurement to it simply including Logistics. Very few people recognise that the supply chain not only encapsulates these functions but also starts with planning and continues through to the execution of production operations, repair and maintenance.

The process starts with the business defining the level of material they require. They have immediate control over the part that is ordered for direct consumption and are central to establishing and approving inventory levels for the material held in stock. Since this demand generates a requirement for significant quantities of material (across production, projects and planned maintenance shutdowns etc.) the power and perception of the procurement function are artificially enlarged despite being essentially limited to achieving lowest bid negotiations. In some organisations, the Contracting and Procurement team is responsible for the material management itself and, consequently, most improvement initiatives are focused on the cost of the material rather than the improvement, resilience and sustainability of the entire supply chain. In addition to this, the very nature of the organisational structure means that the supply chain is operated in a silo manner. Supply chain knowledge and innovation are fundamentally undermined by this fixation on unit cost and silo working. Suppliers are often treated as a second-class party in this relationship with the Oil and Gas companies who take great pride in defining detailed specifications resulting in bespoke and 'gold plated' equipment and material requirements.

There are national and global standards bodies in industries such as automotive, healthcare and aerospace that allow suppliers to standardise resulting in cost optimisation. In the oil and gas sector there are only national bodies and no global standards. The absence of them results in bespoke specifications which can drive an added premium of 60% upwards.

Next to procurement the other major supply chain function, Logistics, sits within the supply chain but is not the entire supply chain despite the perception often held by operations leadership. Logistics is focussed on the movement of people and material, using land, marine and air transport. We have observed that often Logistics may be assigned the task of storing material and warehouse management thus a larger part of the supply chain. However, within the warehouse or supply depots where the functions meet, procurement and logistics may easily duplicate efforts or create multiple internal billing operations due to poorly defined and executed

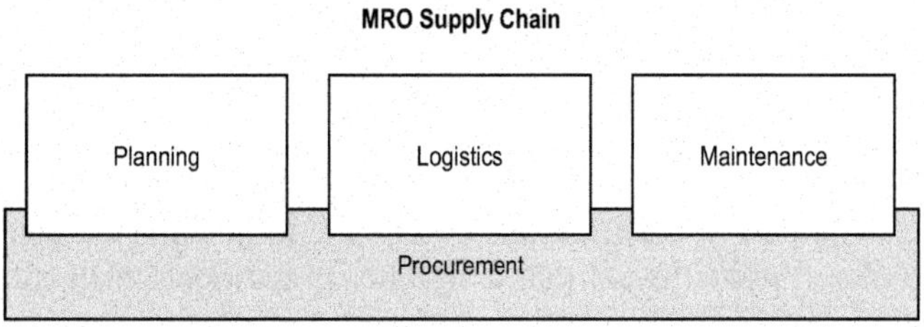

Fig. 3.3 The MRO procurement

interfaces. Figure 3.3 shows how procurement needs to support the three key pillars of the MRO Supply Chain.

The ability to drive improvements as an industry requires a considerable coordinated effort. As an example, the automotive industry has standards across all of its elements of design, production, lifetime production and maintenance. Today it is a significant challenge to achieve this in the O&G industry. It is very interesting to observe that in this sector there are many and varied levels of joint ventures between oil majors (IOC) and the national ministries (NOC) and yet when it comes to standardisation it is severely limited if it exists at all. They all approach their operations as well as the maintenance of the asset in their own unique way. At the time of crew change or shift change as is common in many of the joint ventures, the teams operate in a way that is native to their own IOC. You can imagine the disruption, lack of continuity and often contradictory choices and decisions that are put in motion. In reality, the teams are actually doing their best, in accordance with their key performance indicators and performance measurement. Often these standards are specific to the IOC as they have developed over a period. This results in a spiral effect where the complexity drives variability in the supply chain and these variabilities in turn impact performance and cost, leading to lack of reliability along with the interfaces of the supply chains.

Most IOCs have a formidable Procurement function. With billions to spend, this function prides itself in managing the spending of the company. The opportunity for making savings is based around a principle of 40% based on the specification, 40% on the demand and 20% on the price. Although the procurement teams understand the basic principle of 40:40:20, the business finds it difficult to change its ways on either demand or specification. Therefore, the procurement team is persistently forced to reduce price, at all costs, which re-enforces the silo approach. This constant focus on price undermines the resilience of the supply chain and the vendor to say nothing about the corner cutting or failure to supply which diminishes quality and service. Due to the short-term focus and lack of attention on the lifetime of the system when equipment was procured, today many assets that are ageing, miss critical spare parts and they are also no longer available from the suppliers. This could be a result of the Bill of Material being updated, or the part itself discontinued or upgraded and even in some extreme cases the supplier itself no longer exists. To even get the information on the product required by the Maintenance and the Repair team often will start with a very time-consuming and expensive investigation by the supplier on the part or its equivalent in its currently available form.

Overlaid on this is whether to keep the materials in inventory, which should be tied directly to both the reliability supply and the lead time of procuring new parts. Although the main part of the lead time is the time to manufacture and deliver the material, our observations reveal that a significant additional element to this lead time is the complexities inherent in the procurement process (internal approvals, senior stakeholder approvals, regulatory approvals etc.).

If these delays can be reduced, then there is an opportunity to reduce the overall inventory levels. The impact of procurement decisions extends far beyond the supply chain and is critical to maintenance, repair and operation during the asset lifetime. However, siloed functional approach often impedes decision-making and collaboration that must be put to effect to improve OPEX and asset availability.

Let us illustrate how silo thinking may impact the supply chain. As a case, we can explore the challenge of critical spare parts availability that is fundamental to operational continuity and asset availability. During the time of design and build of an asset, the Engineering and Procurement Contractor (EPC) works with the supplier to define the 'critical spares'. These are defined by suppliers with the best intentions of part or systems performance. Now any asset will typically have many 'systems' that keep it operational. These could be hydraulics, electrical, fuel management etc. and each system will have its own critical spare parts. Now put them all together at the asset level and you have a long list of parts that are marked 'critical'. The position held by both Engineering and Maintenance is often that the Procurement and Material Management teams must hold all critical spares in inventory. This can and does result in containers of spare parts and components that stack up on the site. If it is an offshore operation, then this can consume significant square meters of valuable real estate.

In reality, as an asset age, conditions change, elevating some systems and subsystems to become more important than others. In fact, although some systems may be upgraded the old systems may still remain in place as a contingency. We have observed that despite the change in priorities of these systems and subsystems (up or down), the criticality of the supporting spares is infrequently reviewed and even when they are, it takes great effort and a project team to complete the task. The consequence is that the critical material being held is dated and has significant gaps in it, simultaneously resulting in downtime of the asset and overstock, the worst of both worlds. It is essential that the business recognises a few 'critical' spare parts are more 'critical' than others and that it needs to continuously monitor and update its critical material, holding the most critical closest to the operation and removing from its inventory material less critical.

It is not an uncommon event, despite inventory worth millions, the asset will stop producing because a \$20 gasket was not available. Its procurement and lead time for delivery mean it requires expediting as well as leading to higher cost to replenishment. These events will trigger the usual war rooms, email chains that run into pages and pages, and heightened emotions across board. The engineering team fed up with waiting on orders for the part directly from the supplier will often order more to avoid future shortages. There will be the usual firefighters and the celebrity operator or the manager who manages to get the part and save the day. Functional silos do indeed drive similar narratives of crises and victory in many different flavours.

The way to solve this requires an end-to-end (e2e) perspective. A collaborative environment where the list of critical spares are reviewed on a regular basis and new parts added whilst others are delisted based on operational performance. This allows the procurement team as part of the supply to maintain the right inventory at locations that allow rapid delivery of parts at the point of failure or ensure that the supplier holds the right insurance part or inventory for speedy supply.

We observed that a similar analysis at one of the offshore locations reduced the number of critical systems to 30 from over 600. This was a result of historical failure analysis. From these 30 systems, only 600 spare parts were deemed to be essential for operations continuity. This was a reduction of over 90% from the original list of critical items that required inventory to support the operation. This joint and focussed analysis allowed many parts to be declassified as critical, saving inventory and working capital while improving the availability of the asset.

The only way to prepare and succeed in the current market and deliver resilience in future is to focus on supply chain optimisation that reduces the complexity and demand for materials whilst ensuring security of supply and only then focus on cost reduction. A continuous improvement and optimisation drive towards more preventative maintenance to improve production and operational continuity as opposed to continuous bleeding through an inefficient patchwork of expensive corrective maintenance. It is a recognised fact that running equipment to failure is more costly both in terms of lost production as well as damaging equipment than maintaining it to the set maintenance schedule. Deploying a preventive maintenance strategy in an e2e fashion will drive improved cost and availability performance as illustrated in Fig. 3.4. Further, by increasing preventative maintenance it is often seen that the frequency of corrective maintenance events reduces by a greater percentage, the difference between a well-maintained car versus a poorly maintained one that frequently breaks down! (Fig. 3.5).

The business relies heavily on the supply chain to deliver people, goods and services to the front line to support production continuity and therefore the lifeblood of a successful business is its supply chain, which until recently was the most overlooked function in this industry. So, let us talk more about why this is so.

There Are No External Customers… …just internal operations and if they say, 'we need one, we will buy three! We will allow for one to be out of spec, one to get lost leaving one to use'. Something traditionally heard from maintenance managers.

The supply chain is there to support operations, wells and projects, however, traditionally it has been treated as a function within each of production, wells and

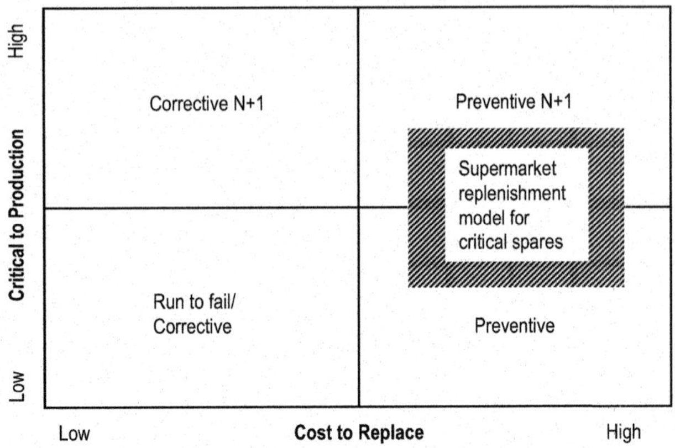

Fig. 3.4 The spare parts strategy (A $N + 1$ operating strategy means there is more capacity in the system than is required and is intended to protect the most critical parts of the organisation. This is described further in the tenth module later in this book.)

projects. This shows that it has never been recognised as its own integrated function but just as an activity, or necessary evil, that involves movement of goods and services.

We see this gap at all levels, at an asset level as well as at an enterprise level. The oil and gas industry does not have a supply chain at the country level and therefore will never have it at corporate level such as other industries. Such is the level importance of the supply chain in the most advanced industries, they have achieved distinct leadership roles such as Chief Supply Chain Officer to manage this function corporately. This is not something we have seen in the Oil and Gas sector.

There is a misconception that price is the only thing that matters. Fundamentally there is no supply chain because there is no integrated and unified goal. Production = availability, Procurement + accountant = money. In turn, this lack of integration leads to an inability to meet the schedule as well as driving significant waste throughout the supply chain (Fig. 3.6).

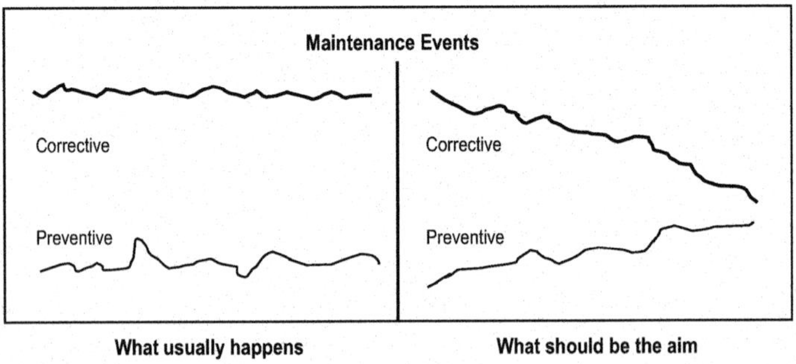

Fig. 3.5 Maintenance strategies

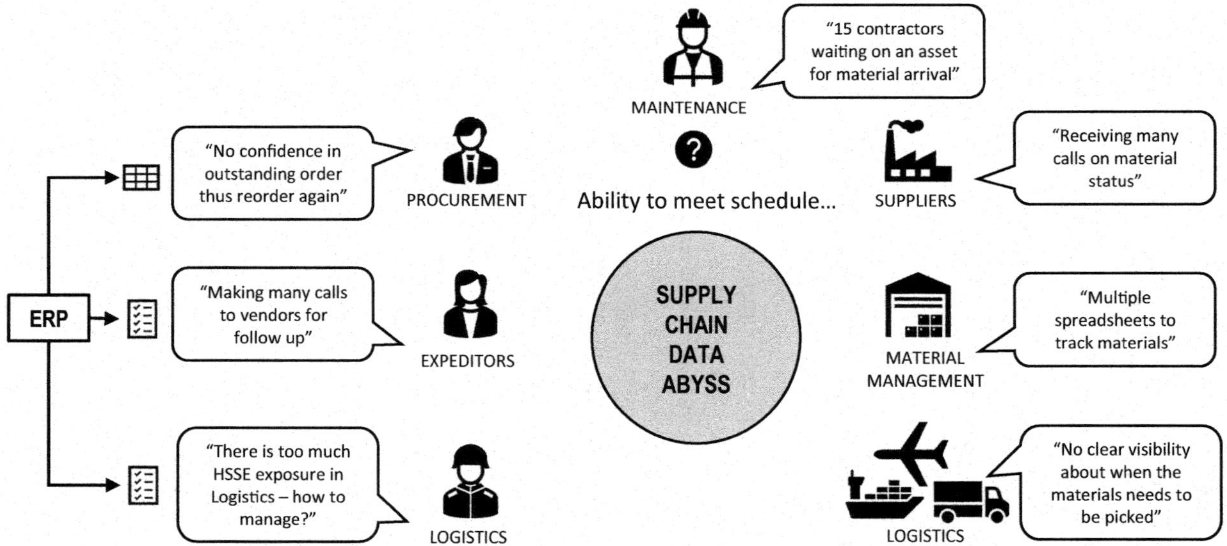

Fig. 3.6 How do our supply chains work today?

3.3 Three Bids and a Buy

Procurement in this industry is an essential function, due to the significant expenditure on equipment and services. This is more so than in many industries because of the multibillion dollar levels of spending. The progression in this area over the recent years has been from a 'three bids and a buy' approach to a much more structured approach to getting a reliable, professional and cost-effective solution to the overall requirement. This has a huge impact on the overall cost performance in this industry.

However, many companies believe this is the sole focus of attention for the supply chain and that improvements in and reductions of cost are the only focus. Consideration of internal reliability and asset availability is often low on the agenda. As such the price might be right but the ability to deliver is not aligned. The procurement leadership given the cost performance has cost performance at its core, however, decisions made solely on cost are not always the best for the business.

It is critical that there is absolute alignment between the strategies of the production function, with the cost objectives of the business and that both of these two elements drive the strategy forward. A supply chain should be driven by the needs of the business, but not just in terms of cost but also in its reliability to deliver.

The three parts shown in Fig. 3.7 must be central to the overall strategy to get the best results. A skewed approach will be suboptimal. The tendency within the organisation is that one of these three parties is more dominant than the other two and therefore the solution is skewed towards either operations, cost or logistics. Typically cost or operations are much more dominant than logistics.

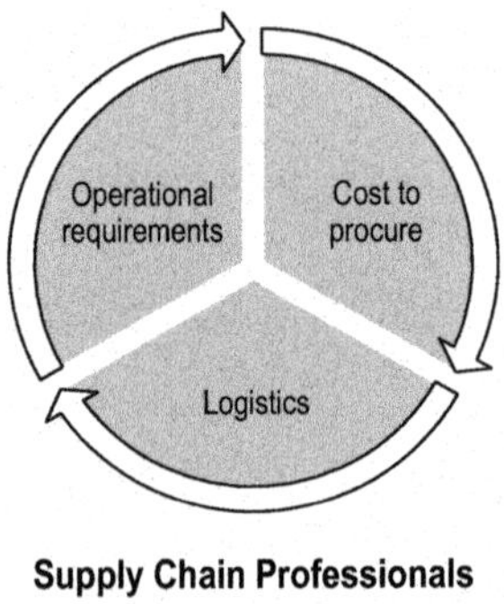

Fig. 3.7 Balancing the corporate strategies

3.4 The Mindset of Waste

Large corporations often roll out initiatives such as Lean and Six Sigma intended to highlight the missed opportunities to reduce waste and to improve performance, whether by removing non-value added activities or encouraging departments to work in a coordinated way or removing complexity. In addition to this, another objective is often to simplify and harmonise performance indicators so all the functions are aligned towards the stated corporate goals, but is this enough?

Figure 3.8 shows the purpose of and difference between Lean and Six Sigma. It is critical that this is understood prior to labelling work with these titles, removing waste in one area without considering how it impacts the end-to-end value chain is not good practice.

As we have observed earlier, some of the more visible waste in this context can be inventory, expediting parts, secret inventory (squirrel stores), interdepartmental billing, poorly stored parts beyond their shelf lives etc. Figure 3.9 shows the eight wastes, including underutilised talent, and it is clear to see where excess inventory, defects and over processing fit in. However, in addition to these, there are some less obvious areas of waste, for instance, due to missing standardisation of parts there is a huge variation in lead times, the time it takes for routine maintenance, distorted plans created on the assumption that it will fail and therefore it does—a genuine self-fulfilling prophecy!

The objectives of Six Sigma (Fig. 3.10) are twofold, firstly to align the average output of the process with the customer promise, ensuring that it at least achieves this goal. The second and arguably more important objective is to reduce the variability of the process, to enable delivery of results closer to the mean. Through these two objectives, the customer will receive what was promised and will receive that consistently.

There are many different types of employees throughout every workforce, people with vastly different experiences and approaches. Some believe they can change the world, and do not get us wrong, some of them are very capable of doing this, but many do not want to change. Change is alien and more importantly it is hard work.

Fig. 3.8 Lean and six sigma

Lean is a strategy for maximising value for the customers	**Six Sigma** is a data driven process improvement methodology.
It is the relentless pursuit of perfect process through **waste elimination** along the entire value stream.	It focuses on **variations** in a process and uses statistical tools to reduce process standard deviation and shift the **mean** towards target.

8 WASTES	PRODUCT FLOW	DATA FLOW
DEFECTS	• Poor quality of materials • Equipment failures • Missing customer due dates – Internal & External	• Personal data in correct • Wrong BOMs • Incorrect Master data • rework
OVERPRODUCTION	• Production that is more than needed or before it is needed. • Sub assemblies and components between feeder and main lines	• Processing before next operation is ready • Making early too early
WAITING	• Wasted time waiting for next step in a process • Operators waiting • Machines waiting	• Waiting for approvals • Process awaiting overnight batch runs
UNDER UTILISED TALENT	• Not applying cross training and skills upgrade across manufacturing cells	• Underutilising people's talent, skills and knowledge
TRANSPORTATION	• Conveyance of any materials tools • Unnecessary movement of products and materials	• Delivering hard copies for archives • Sending hard copies for signature
INVENTORY	• Excess materials and products not being processed • Buffer and safety stocks • Squirrel stores	• Multiple level of approvals in a process • Unnecessary documentation and storage
MOTION	• Unnecessary motion by people • Operators bending, turning, twisting • Machines 'cutting air'	• Navigating multiple screens to input data • Looking for data across multiple excel downloads
EXTRA PROCESSING	• More work or higher quality than required by customer • Planned re-work • Un planned re work	• Duplicate entries • Printing and scanning • Multiple options to enter the same data

Fig. 3.9 The waste in lean

The real question here is, why are they like this? Why do some people put more effort into resisting change than it would have taken to make the change itself?

Consider that people can move between these groups, from eager and open individuals to reluctant to change, with the underlying reason that 'we have tried it before, and it didn't work then' or 'why bother others will stop it from working anyway' through to 'I tried to implement change before and got my fingers burnt'. Aside from the naysayers who believe that this is just another initiative that will be forgotten in a short period of time (and these are bad enough), there are those who have tried to change in the past and not had a pleasant time through it, being penalised in performance assessments for trying to do the right thing and failing or

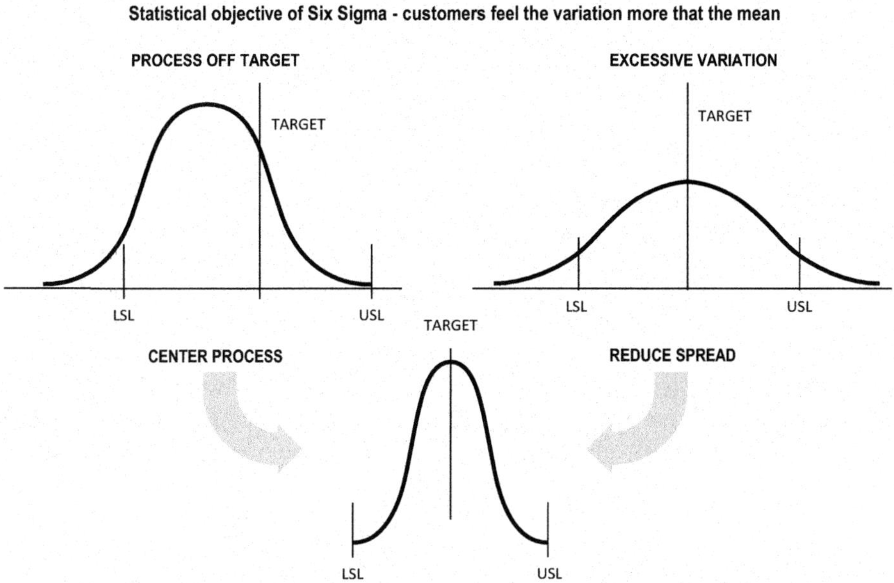

Fig. 3.10 The six sigma objective

helping another department achieve their targets, whilst appearing not to worry about their own goals even when it was the right thing to do. This second group of people can be much more damaging as they typically change the culture of the whole enterprise, not just now but for the future too.

Often, misaligned KPIs are the root of the problem. Leaders want to achieve a personal goal or have a specific emphasis on delivering a set outcome, which might not align with another part of the organisation. This could be a consequence of having an eye on the next job or only considering short-term goals or it could be down to a lack of understanding of the bigger picture or indeed little knowledge of the underlying principle.

Take for instance the situation where a production unit is tasked with maintaining production 'at all cost'. Well, they will be really focused on ensuring that inventory availability will not harm production and so will embark on making sure that everything they think they need is available. Even if they do not really need it, it will be insurance. Later when a different leader is in place, no one knows or remembers why this inventory is here. In fact, often no one knew the inventory was there in the first place. We have observed such a leadership decision to stock 2 years' worth of spares resulted in a massively bloated inventory problem. Years later the rule was still in place though its original intent was long forgotten and no longer relevant. The leader who made the decision moved on and subsequent leaders continued to work with an archaic and OPEX intensive process. The insurance has run out and the viability of the inventory too. This means that what was once working capital now needs to be written off against OPEX, dealing with the error of those who came before.

It is critical that the business, any business, focus on changing the mindset rather than just the process or the system. It is essential that the workforce understands the current business objective and is aligned with it, to recognise waste and challenge paradigms, even if they do not understand well the rationale that put them in place. The leadership should place their trust and forgive mistakes if things do not turn out successfully while making a positive change. This is an essential part of a learning mindset and has to be the mantra adopted throughout the whole organisation.

In the O&G industry, it is not unusual to see procurement creating waste by incurring significant OPEX and working capital costs through unnecessary spending on inventory. Alas, this approach is not limited to procurement, but it is also common to see the same approach in Logistics and Services with the justification of protecting production or ensuring the project delivery schedule is met. Rarely are surplus inventory and resources critical in themselves, but their presence (or availability) is often used to cover for inefficiencies in other areas. This in turn leads to significant waste through Inventory write-off and redundant resources. This inherent distrust on reliability of functional partners has significant financial impacts, either by requesting more resources than is required, or through bypassing the prescribed processes and therefore losing benefits from enterprise level supplier management and negotiations.

All of this has a knock-on effect through the rest of the value stream, it increases pressure on vendors to supply what is not required, it increases expenditure to buy what is not needed and it drives up working capital. This extra inventory contributes nothing to the performance of the business and the material is likely to either deteriorate before it is required or, in the worst case, it will be written off which will impact profitability.

The relationship between the level of inventory and the risk it mitigates is not well understood. The common misconception is that inventory is a guaranteed way of mitigating *all* risk, rather than the understanding that *only* carefully selected inventory mitigates a portion of the risk.

These examples of waste have been observed across the board and in discussion with our peers across IOCs and NOCs.

- *KPIs*—The lack of understanding about an e2e supply chain, or the interdependence of the functions drives a silo mentality, higher costs and poor handovers on the interfaces. Bureaucratic measurement of success within a function drives delays across the e2e process which in turn drives distrust and is at the root of the poor practices leading to a slow and overweight Supply Chain.
- *Process*—Paying for the negligence of previous stocking policies, or at least poor stocking practices. Commercial decisions are based on least cost and not value. When cost of procurement is the prime driver, the potential short-term savings can become outweighed over time by dis-optimisation of the overall supply chain.

- *Urgent requests*—The need to get material quickly is always considered to be more important than getting materials in a coordinated and managed way. Planning is based on a 'here and now' attitude. We need it, therefore we must spend the money to procure it and when this is a just-in-case purchase on the back of a concern rather than a need this drives redundancy in the system. There is little pre-emptive planning to ensure that the issues on the horizon can be spotted early enough to make mitigations and avoid the issue in the first place. There are few (if any) control towers fully deployed in this industry.
- *Scale*—We have observed that in many situations business requirements and the relative cost of the equipment are used as the reason to buy surplus inventory. Renting a rig costs \$200 k per day thus buying spares worth a few millions merits little discussion. During the boom times of oil and gas, OPEX is dwarfed by the value of the oil and gas produced and this habit has been hard to wean off for the industry. With COVID-19, related low oil prices and production restrictions, these poor behaviours have been scrutinised and determined to be the difference between making a profit or making a loss.
- *Commercial objectives*—Driven by cost, vendors push themselves to win the work knowing that if the bid is successful, they will be unsustainable in the medium term (or even in the short term). The vendors bid low, suffer for a short period, then request additional funding. This does not encourage an environment of partnership where participants are looking out for the benefit of the agreement. There is a general mistrust of suppliers who are seen to focus on maximising benefits as opposed to becoming a critical partner for long-term progress and development. Given the lack of common standards defined by a coalition or regional or global guidelines, vendors are encouraged to drive decisions based on the individual tenders rather than create a strategy across the industry from which everyone would benefit.

Chapter 4
The Missing Pieces

4.1 Logistics: An International Tour Operator

The history of Logistics in the Oil and Gas Industry is complex. Given the remote location of assets it includes all modes—Land (ranging from pick-up trucks to large trailers, buses and cranes), Aviation (Rotary and Fixed wings) and Marine (Tugboats, security, houseboats, barges, Jack up barges, PSV, water taxis, flotels) with all its complexities and regulations. All of these modes also include the inherent health and safety (HSSE) exposure and in certain countries security measures. Theft, robbery and armed assault are often part and parcel of asset operations in some geographies.

Unlike the majority of supply chains, logistics in the Oil and Gas sector also includes movement of people and, following COVID challenges, it has been expanded to include Hotels, Transit canters, Quarantine layovers and much more. Thus, the typical oil and gas supply chain not only concerns itself with material movements but is effectively equivalent to a tour operator as well! If you add to the mix the complexity of expat contractors, it becomes an international tour operation dealing with visas, government regulations and restrictions, and back-to-back schedules.

Metrics define actions and with all the inherent complexities, the primary purpose of logistics remains to deliver material and people to the assets on time at any cost. Upstream business measurement typically is based on Material on Time (MOT) whereas the Downstream business measurement is On Time In Full (OTIF). Neither of these measures the efficiency of the supply chain. The metrics are designed to serve the immediate needs of the assets which are trying to maximise or meet daily production targets and as far as the asset team is concerned, that is *all* that matters. To add to the grief, sadly there is constant rhetoric and comparison with online retail giants which is not useful for the team members where the supply routes are complex and long. We have become used to the service level, ease of order and track and trace

S. Roy, S. Dunbar, *Improving Supply Chains in the Oil and Gas Industry*, Springer Series in Supply Chain Management 16,
https://doi.org/10.1007/978-3-030-95066-8_4

of online retailers and expect the same level and quality of service without investing in any of the infrastructures that would make it possible.

Another illustration of a misleading and unhelpful metric is helicopter utilisation based on the number of seats paid for by the business rather than number of people sitting in the helicopter for each flight. This measurement was designed to meet a functional KPI (cost recovery) rather than end-to-end cost optimisation (resource utilisation). This changed when helicopter availability became low due to recent industry crises amongst the helicopter operators and the focus turned to resource utilisation. Similar challenges are endemic across all modes of transport and resources, for instance, the maintenance of a fleet of pickup trucks and grab trucks (i.e. with hydraulic loading arms), which are often kept on standby for any request for parts or components from the asset. We have observed a single drum of lubricants being delivered on a pick-up truck. Little thought is given to creating a 'milk run' route between the assets where possible to reduce the fleet size, related fuel consumption and resource requirement. These concepts are common in the retail industry and do not require much effort to adopt.

Referring to an earlier section—a supply chain "designed" by engineers has delivered a solution which may be a functional working supply chain as per the specification but have little consideration towards an efficient supply chain operation, that may put priority on end-to-end cost optimisation and reducing the working capital (inventory) required to meet service requirements. Unfortunately, we observed that the focus has been on prioritizing delivery service towards asset availability at any costs. There are very few real supply chain experts in the ecosystems and we (author's opinion) do not believe procurement and the category managers to be supply chain experts. Lately, we have observed that realising the importance of supply chain, procurement has rebranded itself to supply chain in IOCs. Recognition and adoption of the identity is a step in the right direction, however, unless true supply chain experts are put in the leadership role little fundamental change will be made. Thus, supply chains in this industry will miss an opportunity for a step-change improvement in performance, limited by the rate of process evolution based on experience gained.

But that is not all—so far, we have talked from a cost lens. Very little is driven from a demand angle. Logistics needs to know the demand presented by the asset operations, but they also need to be able to influence the demand to optimise cost. During the course of a turnaround campaign offshore, we observed that the logistics project teams were set in the sequence that they needed to follow as per the project plan. However, this sequence required two accommodation vessels to be mobilised for a four-week period. The mobilisation costs for these vessels were significant. Through the intervention of the logistics marine team, it was possible to influence the timing of the project work execution. This removed the requirement for the overlap in accommodation vessels and allowed the use of a single vessel for both of these campaigns. This effective dialogue illustrates the power of enabling those who understand the 'cost to service ratio', which operates at an end-to-end level of operations versus delivery of a discreet project or activity.

The above case study is again a reflection of historical evolution of the function which is primarily designed to respond to the requirements and not necessarily be part of the optimisation process together with the asset operations. This is made even more complex when you consider that the operations across Assets, Wells and Projects can each have their own logistics functions (including contractors and EPCs suppliers).

4.2 Planning: Splendid Isolation?

Typically, Oil and Gas companies are very good at planning projects, focussing on cradle to grave asset planning with little attention to operational execution planning. The expertise focuses specifically on getting them from the concept through the relevant decision gates to execution, with the supporting functions expected to fall into line and deliver them. Significant energy is focussed here to ensure a successful project level outcome. However, our experience is that little energy is given to a coordinated plan, one that encompasses the projects, wells and maintenance aspects in the business. It is the equivalent of 'build it and they will come' but it is not done in a way that will be efficient for the future.

Operational planning existed but in siloes. Functions such as projects, wells and maintenance created their own limited plans, which do cover elements of the supply chain (especially logistics), which resulted in discreet plans even at the logistics level. This has led to duplication, overcapacity and inefficient contracts being the norm. Not only were the rates not optimised, in some instances, functions went into a bidding contest against each other driving up the rates even further. The vendors naturally took advantage of the left hand not knowing what the right hand was doing. The lack of a cohesive plan naturally leads to suboptimal execution. Surprisingly this still exists in most Oil and Gas assets.

When setting out on a journey, it is a good idea to know where your destination is and to plot out the journey for all involved. However, in Oil and Gas the functional teams continue to develop their own roadmaps and plans. There is a gap in the organisational structure whose role is to unify the plans, standing on both sides of production and supply chain to recognise and align priorities to genuinely drive availability gains.

There is a desire to be like Amazon in the Oil and Gas industry getting the benefits of visibility and traceability, but this goal completely misses the need for the process to start with aligned, excellent planning upfront.

Fail to Plan? Then Plan to Fail! In response to the Low Oil Price (LOPR) there has been a significant effort across operating units to reduce their cost. The initial part of this exercise has been fairly easy. Identify cost components, create a pipeline of opportunities and set rhythm and discipline of weekly cadence to ensure that value opportunities are matured and delivered and captured in the financial systems. However, once you have scraped the fat and trimmed the low-hanging fruits the exercise requires end-to-end collaboration across functional teams to get the next level of saving. This alignment is critical to address the inefficiencies that build up in the value stream as each function overcompensates to achieve their own goals and objectives. Evidence of this is where the Wells' team arranges their own supply of materials to meet their delivery performance, Procurement creates their own Cost improvement targets, planned major maintenance projects concentrate all their activities in the first half of the year as they plan to fail, with little trust in supply chain delivering material on time.

This is deep rooted and perhaps the biggest vulnerability of the supply chains in Oil and Gas companies. The scale makes it easier for the inefficiencies to continue, as these supply chains are big in themselves, but the opportunity for making significant improvements through integration and alignment is also huge.

A good start would be to resolve the planning issue which will address the giant hairball of a problem. There are multiple plans across logistics, wells and operations. For example, instead of tactical management of over 200 vessels, the specific effort behind proper planning will optimise the demand (fleet size), maximise service (availability) and have a much bigger impact on the cost than negotiations alone. This creates a much more sustainable business and prevents the vendors from coming back and saying they cannot deliver on agreed prices because in reality they were unrealistic in the first place. In order to keep the ecosystem strong and effective, we can and should help the suppliers become business partners, instead of pushing them to bankruptcy. A case in point highlight would be the bankruptcy of many helicopter service providers, through inefficient planning that had created a capacity based on seat utilisation. That meant that booking of seats ensured that seat utilisation was always very high. However, here was the hidden inefficiency, booking the seats does not mean someone actually travelled! The helicopters would depart with booked but empty seats. With the cost pressure, the focus went on ensuring people actually travelled only when required or faced penalties for no-shows. Suddenly the bookings dropped, and a good part of the helicopter fleet went on standby as overcapacity. Naturally with high cost of maintenance, pilots, crews and infrastructures meant that many suppliers started to file for bankruptcy. A double whammy, as oil and gas companies were faced with fewer suppliers who were far more demanding and an increased risk to operational continuity, if the crew or urgent materials could not be delivered on time to the asset.

4.3 Integration: A Rare Commodity?

Working without a single plan drives significant effort and resources to ensure alignment across plans, which in turn becomes the primary activity adding little value to the enterprise. By using a single plan and investing this time and effort into

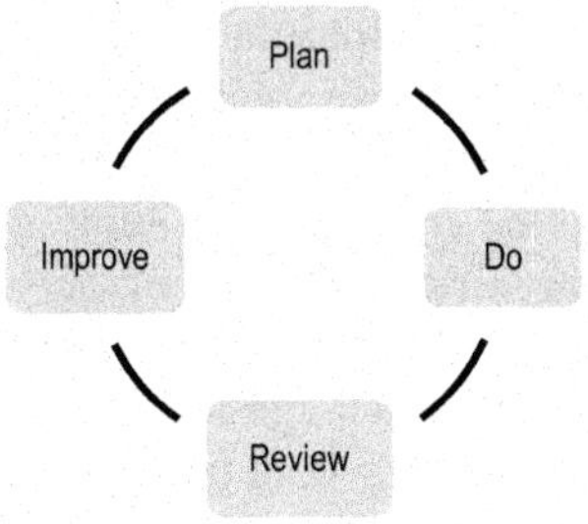

Fig. 4.1 The continuous improvement cycle

optimization and streamlining drives real value at the beginning rather than trying to recover value at the end.

If you miss the good foundation of planning upfront most of your energy will go into Cost recovery at the end. This is where Cost Improvement targets become the primary KPI of the procurement team. There is little bandwidth left for effective contract performance tracking and continuous improvement initiatives because this focuses on the symptoms, not the root cause.

The well-known illustration in Fig. 4.1 has a simple insight. The less time you invest in Planning, the more time needs to be spent in Doing and Reviewing and hardly if any in Improving. That is why Taiichi Ohno from Toyota would always maintain that we must plan long and then act fast. Insufficient time and energy in the planning phase results in significant time and energy in the doing phase to simply deliver required expectations. This in turn drives a behaviour to 'get the job done' versus what it should be to 'get the job done efficiently'. As a consequence, there is a business culture where the 'firefighters' are rewarded and good planning is viewed as 'just part of your job', it will not win you medals or recognition. When in reality the focus should be the other way around since great planning significantly removes the need for firefighting.

Recognising people at the moment and not for their preparation is neither an effective nor sustainable way of working. A popular Bollywood movie scene has a great illustration of this where a successful businessman drives his car into a garage. He looks at the mechanic and asks if he can fix it. The mechanic looks under the hood for a while and then picks a small hammer and taps it on one of the mechanical parts and voila—the problem is fixed. The businessman is very pleased and asks for the bill. The hero says a thousand rupees, a very significant amount in the 1970s when the film was made. The businessman is aghast and loses his cool. 'You are charging me a thousand rupees to tap a hammer once?' he shouts incredulously. Indeed, our hero, the mechanic, calmly looks at him and remarks, 'You are right, it cost you 5 rupees for the hammer tap and the other nine hundred and ninety-five rupees to know exactly where to tap!' What a triumph of knowledge and wit. It became folklore for generations. Though a nice story, it contains a powerful message for organisations. Experience and talent are developed over years. If someone makes tasks look simple and executes it efficiently, do not cloud your perception and conclude that this is easily done thus naturally low value add. Take time to understand. There might be numerous 'fires' that the skilled operators are avoiding with ease, but they never get the due recognition for it. As previously said, organisations often reward last-minute crises solvers but not the one who prevent crises from occurring in the first place.

In some organisations, it is believed that people's development is more important than knowledge retention. This plays into multiple reorganisations where continuously refreshing talent bleeds experience. It is not uncommon for an employee to be subjected to a major reorganisation every 18 months or so.

In a departmental meeting, recognition was sought and given for a significant contract being delivered. Praise and accolades were given to the team involved in this achievement. However, the question of 'When' this contract should have been delivered was never asked, it was over a year late. The team missed an opportunity to learn from this event like in so many others in the past. Poor planning in this instance meant that the deadlines were missed, and we spent all the time 'doing', there was no time for 'reviewing' and improving. This was further exacerbated by giving recognition after delivery rather than following it all through to review and improve.

This type of approach basically shortcuts the process to Plan and Do whilst at the same time condoning the extension of the timeline. Sadly, we keep on repeating this pattern over and over again. Rinse and Repeat, rarely, if ever, taking the time to step back and review. As an industry that leads in 'Causal Analysis' of engineering failures we do not apply the same rigour to supply chain failures. This drives a 'who is to blame?' culture rather than a 'learning organisation' and further reinforces siloed mentality.

This mentality drives a vicious circle through functional point scoring and localised praise, rather than a virtuous circle with shared goals and improvement agenda. We have observed the community of Wells engineers, proudly carrying the label 'we are tribal' on their shoulders. Wells delivery scored the highest performance, however, not from the perspective of the asset they were meant to serve, leaving in their wake excess inventory, premature handovers driving ongoing corrective actions necessary by the asset.

4.4 Does Sales and Operations Planning Really Work in Oil and Gas?

In most consumer industries, a sales forecast is the trigger point for all manufacturing and procurement activities. It includes the impact of promotions, the launch of new products and changes in price points but is based on effectively predicting what the market will do under various circumstances, market dynamics are influenced by events and activities which are outside the control of the organisation. This is normally managed through a Sales and Operations Planning (S&OP) process (Fig. 4.2).

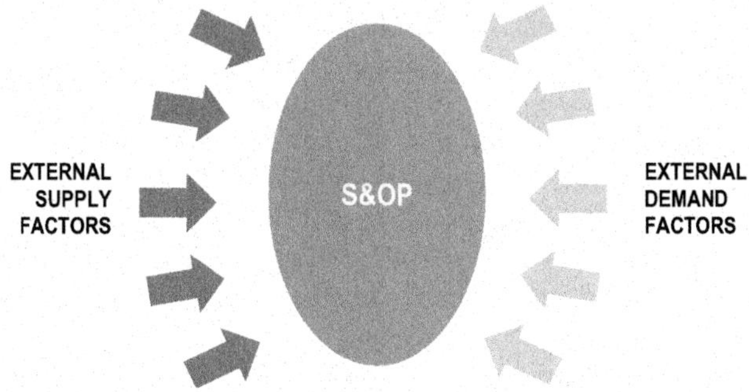

Fig. 4.2 Influences on the S&OP planning process

In contrast, an MRO supply chain in the oil and gas industry has complete control of the demand side of the planning process. But it does not have total control over the inbound materials or supply of resources, thus is bound by prevailing market conditions (Fig. 4.3). Ultimately, in oil and gas, there should be more control over internal demand than the FMCG has over their sales. But additional control is neither recognised nor effectively managed. In the Oil and Gas industry, we have a 'known' set of demands as against a demand with inherent 'variations'. Thus, the only reason we should hold inventory in Oil and Gas is to manage the variability of the inbound supply. Any inventory to manage the demand variability should be unacceptable, though it is a common practise.

The belief that an easier and more controllable supply chain has a better chance of succeeding is incorrect. The reason being that freedom to exercise discretion without the necessary alignment and controls ultimately fails to satisfy expectations and

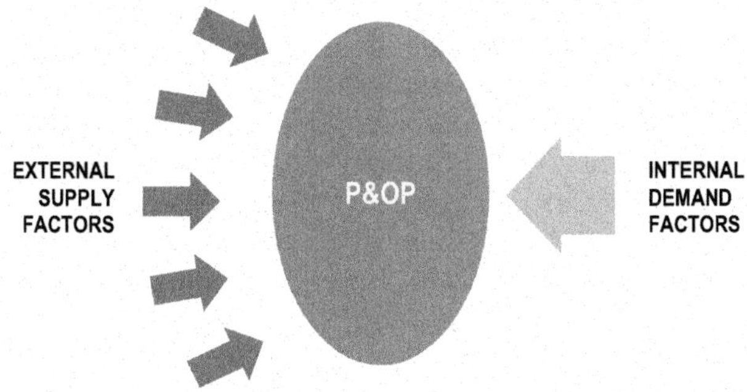

Fig. 4.3 Influences on the P(roduction) &OP planning process

causes unnecessary disruption throughout the value chain. Control and manage strictly this internal interference and success becomes much more likely.

In fresh food supply chains, not only is demand highly variable (salad on hot days, BBQ on sunny days etc.) but also the supply is also highly variable because of its short lead times and its dependencies on other factors such as weather. However, the design of the fresh food supply chain relies heavily on solving all issues within a period of 24 h or less. Thus, there is no cumulative effect, tomorrow is another day with another set of challenges. In order to manage these restrictions, strict controls and processes are in place and understood by everyone in the supply chain. The aligned understanding of the ultimate goal allows the supply chain to focus on delivery rather than managing and investing time and effort into failure management.

In the Oil and Gas MRO supply chain, the less variable demand and more forgiving delivery service should improve cost and service but in actual fact serve as fundamental obstacles in this delivery. This is because the whole supply chain is based on a wide latitude of parameters. If an order is received today, scheduled for delivery tomorrow, as in fresh food distribution, this requires a very focused operating model. It is essential that Oil and Gas adopt more of this type of approach to drive a step change in performance, but to achieve this there has to be a significant change in behaviour.

For some reason, the oil and gas industry misses this insight of the significant advantage it has with a fixed and stable demand that can be internally adjusted or modified to keep the cost and thus the OPEX low. In fact inventory is used increasingly to manage the demand planning inefficiencies. The resultant excess inventory usually falls in no man's land. The Functions do not own it, Procurement does not own it, the asset does not own it and it appears as a line item or working capital (i.e. in asset) in the financial ledgers rather than a liability that it will become an excess or obsolete stock.

The S&OP process is not directly transferable to MRO supply chains but should be modified to take advantage of the Planning and the demand stability that is within the controls of the organisation, thus creating an updated Production and Operations Planning (P&OP) process. This new P&OP process needs to be cognisant of the controls required to take full advantage of the relatively stable demand profile whilst having the primary objective for asset availability and production continuance. Change management and control are critical in ensuring that decisions are made which consider the impact across the entire value chain, rather than biased towards one specific series of objectives from one area in the value chain (See Fig. 3.7 Balancing the corporate strategies in Sourcing and Procurement).

4.5 It Starts with the End in Mind

For a plan to have any chance of success, it is essential that we start with the end in mind. By understanding the destination, the plan to get there is much easier to visualise and create. As a minimum, the parties involved should all be aligned with this end goal (see later defining where you want to be—the North Star), however, for a fully integrated plan, the parties should have an understanding of the impacts on and the opportunities between each of them: where is it possible to align to be more efficient; in a situation where resources are constrained whose need is greater etc.

We need a common goal and a unified plan that everyone understands and is committed to delivering. Making time to create the plan is more important than firefighting to execute and recognition should be focussed on good planning.

So, what is a Good Plan?
A good plan is strategic, it is common across all functions, and it has an understandable goal that can be easily translated into functional requirements. It is not only about ‘where’ you want to go but also ‘how’ and ‘when’ you want to go there. It is measurable and has relevant leading indicators to show progress being made. Probably the most important of all, it is co-created.

It is critical for a good plan to recognise its interdependencies. In the organisation, a major maintenance schedule was created to be delivered in the first 6 months of the year. From a supply chain perspective, this was going to be difficult to deliver both in terms of resource levels and in terms of material availability. When enquired why the plan could not be level loaded throughout the year, it became apparent that it had been built to allow for slippage and catch up in the second half. Thus, the plan was designed with ‘failure’ as a key driver. Rather than planning in case of failure, this approach guaranteed failure. At the root of this mindset is a lack of understanding of end-to-end supply chain, lack of integrated plan, a lack of co-owned interdependent plan and insufficient challenge back from supply chain, because this is always how we have done it (Rinse and repeat as mentioned before).

To reiterate a good plan is understandable, aligned, co-created and recognises interdependencies. It also needs to have a commitment to its delivery from all levels within the business, people helping people to deliver not simply cascading what they should do.

Who owns the plan?
Plans must have their origins in the need of the business to sustain, improve and grow. However, that does not mean that the plan is owned by the ‘business’. It has to be owned ‘across’ the business with a genuine shared ownership. It is not a top-down plan, even though this is how it is always treated. It should be built from the bottom-up to meet the business objectives. Thus, whilst the business ‘owns’ the objectives, the plan to ‘deliver’ the objective is owned across the functions and co-created.

The plan should not only be about what we deliver but it should also include when we deliver and how we deliver. The element that is missing in almost all plans is ‘how’ we deliver. The normal method of communication is to cascade the plan which assumes a master–servant deployment, rather than having a genuine engagement and co-creation process to ensure alignment and buy-in to it.

Successful planning is inherently an agile activity. It makes continuous improvements in small steps towards the business objectives. It does not wait for a quarterly or half-yearly set piece for planning only to realise that we may have to backtrack and change course to remain aligned with the business objectives and their delivery. It should take the form of continuous planning with quarterly, and half-yearly points used only for reviewing and adjusting the forward plan rather than being a post-mortem of what the team has been busy with to date. This is often the case and teams burn hundreds of hours preparing for these sessions with leadership which adds little value to the end objective other than to keep them informed. This creates significant 're-work' in the process rather than using learnings to improve future phases. It is about embracing failure to drive opportunities that will improve future delivery.

The plan should have multifunctional ownership to deliver a single set of objectives, embracing failure to make future delivery stronger. To illustrate this, I was in a meeting and after weeks of planning for it we had the entire leadership of a division in a room. We made a good strong case for empowering the frontline where the key role of the leaders was not to have all the answers but to create an environment for the frontline where the teams can suggest and implement new ideas to improve the task, process and business results. As part of the Coaching Masterclass, this seemed to have the right traction with the leaders present, so we tested the waters asking them, how did they feel about allowing their teams to fail? At one point, perhaps to make a comment or have his voice heard, one of the senior leaders remarked that he is in total support of the idea and will allow the teams to fail, no problem, BUT he would only tolerate them to fail once! The next failure will have serious consequences. As a coach, in the room, I realised how much work we still had ahead of us in terms of changing the culture. The whole point of accelerating change by taking away the fear of failure is not well understood in an environment where failure of parts or processes can have a disastrous impact on people's lives or the environment.

To be safe and avoid failures is ingrained deep in the culture and it is all encompassing. To compartmentalise it and change the attitude in some functions while keeping the safety protocols intact will require us to recognise that radical improvements will come from trying new ideas and ways of working. Failure is an essential part of this learning process and can be achieved without jeopardising control or safe working practices. We only need to count the number of times SpaceX landed a rocket wrong and exploded it (safely) before they got it right.

Chapter 5
Twelve Modules for Supply Chain Transformation

5.1 The 12 Modules

The biggest challenge for most supply chains is to create a repeatable process that runs effectively with minimal interventions and is capable of resilience within planned parameters. In most consumer-facing industries, significant effort is invested in designing resilience based on the variability of demand.

In our work over a period of 18 months, we understood that close collaboration with asset maintenance and engineering can narrow the demand pattern for critical spares making them more predictable. As the reliability in specific categories within the supply chain improved this principle could be extended to include planning for additional categories over longer horizons (ultimately moving from 1 to 3 years). Increased collaboration with the Integrated Planning team as well as Logistics thorough weekly/monthly cadence only served to make the process more robust. As supply reliability increases, the noise from the value stream reduces allowing the team to put more attention on event planning such as shutdowns, drilling sequences and projects as well as dealing with genuine emergencies.

We can identify 12 modules of supply chain transformation that helped us deliver a remarkable improvement in the supply chain, which often seemed impossible to fix (Fig. 5.1). There is no set sequence in the deployment of the modules however all of them serve to draw a common thread across the value stream. Although they can be implemented in any order, it is critical that the end user focus and attention to planning are considered early in the process. Any supply chain transformation should remain cognisant of them as they focus on their own gaps/opportunities.

The core concept is based on data flow in one direction (asset through to supplier) and material flow in the other (supplier to asset). The fundamental principle is that this should be as seamless as possible with all attention focussed around removing waste in these flows. For us to be a truly agile supply chain we should be able to spot the inefficiencies fast allowing swift and direct mitigations. This requires KPI's

S. Roy, S. Dunbar, *Improving Supply Chains in the Oil and Gas Industry*, Springer Series in Supply Chain Management 16,
https://doi.org/10.1007/978-3-030-95066-8_5

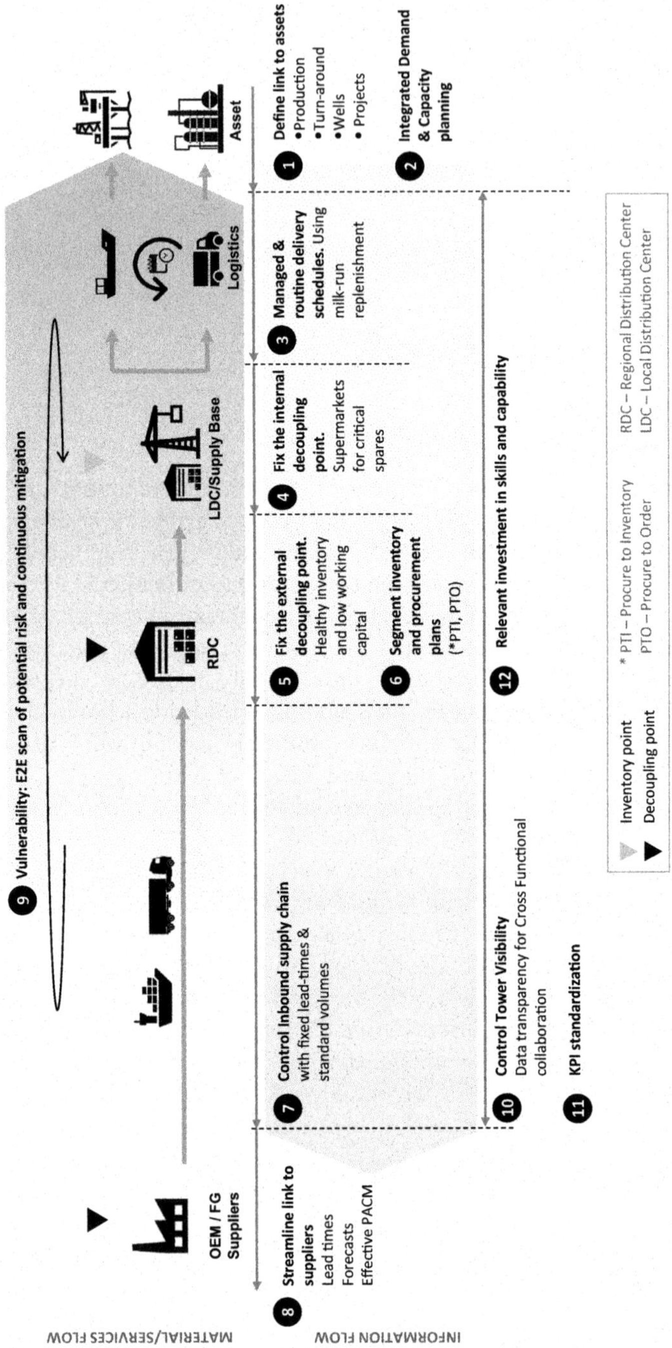

Fig. 5.1 The 12 modules for supply chain transformation

focussed on leading indicators to enable prevention rather than lagging that can only ever enable reviews. We should build our dashboards and control towers based on these as a single source of truth across the value stream.

The concept of Plan-Source-Deliver for a supply chain is robust but has its limitations since it uses a functional lens on the value stream. The primary purpose of any supply chain is to deliver in full what is required, when it is required and at the optimal cost, rather than at the lowest cost. It is critical that the ability of the asset to produce is not undermined by tactical response to minimise cost in the short term.

Here are the 12 modules starting with the information flow.

5.1.1 Define the Link with the Asset

There is a legacy of assets getting what they want. Historically if they have not got what they wanted through the correct methods—they bypass and place direct delivery orders. Through bypassing procurement and using direct charge mechanisms they often buy more than they need to make sure they get what they want and also ensure that in future they are not let down by procurement. Thus, creating their own personal insurance or 'squirrel store'.

The assets have an expectation that it should be like ordering from the internet. 'I place an order and you (procurement) must deliver'. There is a fundamental gap between their appreciation of what can actually be delivered against what they are demanding.

All of the above leads to distrust in the supply chain for materials (and services), even though these supply chains are integral to the success of asset operations. There remains a functional divide and a missing recognition that supply chain is an extension of asset operation whose primary objective is to be a reliable partner for them and contribute to value improvements, not just by better contracts but delivering reliably on time with the lowest working capital possible. To reach this integration across functional divide we need to overcome two things:

(a) The recognition that the operations are a full-fledged member of the supply chain
(b) Identify and remediate gaps in the supply chain delivery capability.

The *wells* function traditionally operated by themselves in isolation because they were a discipline in their own right. Their services were contracted by an asset. They would go in—do their job and leave. To ensure efficiency or their own KPIs for delivery, they would prefer to control all aspects of material and service delivery and not rely upon any other (supply chain) function. To ensure failsafe delivery of long lead time items, ordering excess is almost a standard practice. There is today probably no single asset globally where there are not tons of materials or kilometres of tubular left behind as evidence of this malpractice.

With the cost of rig rentals being in the region of many tens or hundreds of thousands of dollars per day, the wells team can always justify having waste of excess inventory to prevent downtime. However, downtime is rarely solely caused by material non-availability. These behaviours have driven actions that have continually resulted in excess inventory across this industry. Looking over towards *projects* the situation is even worse as the majority of large projects buy their material via an EPC as part of a lump sum contract. This is open to a number of issues:

- Poor handover from the project team to an asset leading to material ending up in no-man's lands between the two.
- Limited record-keeping of what should have been handed over, the project team is too busy with the next new project to worry about the one almost completed, and the operational team is too busy trying to make it work—move forward, do not look back.
- Little consideration of material already in the business or left over from previous projects, the next project team wants to buy new rather than use what already is in inventory, thus creating a significant amount of excess.
- Poor visibility of what is actually surplus even if we can see it physically. As it has already been capitalised, this inventory is not visible in the ERP systems for the teams to use which then propagates the problem. Eventually, it has to be written off, but no one really wants to as it may come in "handy" sometime! There are inventories lying at assets unused for 15+ years under this misconception, incurring cost in terms of storage and preservation—if they are not preserved, they will be unusable anyways.
- There is a belief that every project should hand over 2 years of running spares. The target outcome is that for 2 years we have no need to purchase additional spares. However, we have seen that if these materials are consumed, they do not create demand signals, creating incorrect replenishment levels to accommodate this newly deployed project and therefore inventory is likely not to keep pace with the demand for these materials causing availability issues down the line. The other observation is that these spares put in place as part of the project are not handed over properly and are not visible to the asset resulting in the asset buying new spares during the first 2 years, ultimately leading to a write off from the original project procured inventory.

The major *planned maintenance* cycle is a critical activity to ensure operational longevity of the asset. This activity is known in advance and should be part of the 2/3-year plan. However, planning is often last-minute, which puts undue pressure on the procurement team and results in unnecessary 'rush orders' and their associated costs plus increased workload. Often these expectations are unrealistic and cannot be met and the plan is delayed to a latter part of the year. An appreciation that a level-loaded plan with an understanding of procurement lead time is a foundation towards timely execution.

5.1.2 *Implement Integrated Demand and Capacity Planning*

In order to have an effective and efficient operation, there needs to be a clear goal, and everyone needs to be aligned and bought into that objective. The Oil and Gas industry has a lack of appreciation of who the customer is and therefore a traditional S&OP process is difficult to visualise and execute.

Historically, the business has recognised that all functions need to be on the same page with the same plan, but in its usual way it has failed to actually engage effectively with the relevant functions to ensure an overarching integrated plan is the end result rather than many plans being the trigger point for integration and as a stimuli for all function to pull together their supporting plans. In reality, typically the plan contained where we wanted to get to, but the how and who did what was omitted. The organisation was genuinely trying to do the right thing but without the ability to enable the flow of information this resulted in a suboptimal execution plan leading to mistrust and ultimately failed to execute them effectively.

The planning horizon is multi-faceted with a long-, medium- and short-term perspectives. The long term is typically well aligned with the overall business goals for the assets, with a cradle to grave approach for each production asset. However, the continual refinement of the medium-term plan moves further away from the long-term objective and therefore gets diluted the closer it gets to the short term either because of break-ins (late changes) or from financial pressures, which no longer allow the plan to be executed as expected.

Starting with an aligned set of targets, the business can work on the aligned plans to deliver them as well as optimising the capacity plans within the functions. An example of this is shown in Fig. 5.2, where optimising against an aligned plan can deliver significant benefits in Logistics.

There is a gap between the aims and objectives of the long-term strategic plan and the more immediate pressures and influences when transitioning into the medium and short term. This means that unless there is an agile and robust medium-term planning process, the expectation of the original plan will drive waste into the supply chain due to the changing nature of the shorter-term pressures. This further exacerbates the mistrust in the supply chain to deliver what is required and therefore drives additional 'contingency' behaviours by the business.

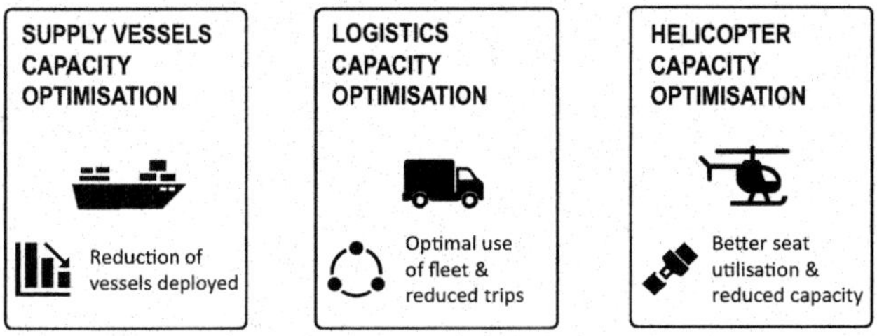

Fig. 5.2 Delivering value across the supply chain logistics

Although it is critical that all plans are aligned, it is critical that they are agile in responding to the immediate pressure as they move towards the point of execution. This issue can be alleviated through a number of approaches:

1. Ensure all functions are aligned and bought into the plan at the start.
2. Listen to the feedback from all functions who need to critique the plan to make it more robust. A good example of this is the 2 Flotels planned in the North Sea which by altering the sequence of the work resulted in only requiring 1 flotel and removing the significant additional mobilisation and demobilisation costs.
3. Measure the reasonableness of the plan (is it too front-end loaded, where are the capability pinch points, can the assets manage this level of work etc.)
4. Monitor on a frequent basis the plans against any changes to the base assumption used in building it and adjust accordingly.
5. Ensure there is a contingency plan in place for the critical elements of the original plan (refer to "Vulnerability").

Figure 5.3 shows how a single point of supply chain planning simplifies processes and enables the deployment of more robust KPIs (see module 11). An integrated demand plan will consider the demand requirements from all the assets and is also multi-year in dimension. Similar to the S&OP process, it is reviewed at the leadership level and signed off every quarter with the latest updates and deviations. On a monthly and weekly basis, the working team is making sure that the demand is updated with any minor changes and in conjunction the supply plans are kept robust. Figure 5.4 shows the main steps to achieving an aligned plan. Unlike the consumer industry where the Marketing and commercial teams are looking into the crystal ball and advanced forecasting to define the future, in Oil and Gas, this can be relatively easy as the Operating Units have a static asset and the life, age, replacement of parts and systems are known well in advance (well, in theory anyway).

There are four key stages in driving an integrated demand and capacity plan across the operating unit.

1. Segment the supply chain horizontally by Value/Consumption matrix. Low value/High-Consumption materials such as stationery, safety gloves etc. should have a different procurement channel. These are Procure to Inventory Items (PTI) which should be routed through a low touch/automated channel. This creates more capacity for items in the High Value/Long Lead time group that requires tendering. These are our Procure to Order (PTO) items. Refer to Module 6, later in this book.
2. Ensure there is a Supply Chain planner in place (we have observed that this role, although common in most industries, is missing in O&G). This is different from Activity Planning baked in Wells, Turn Around and Maintenance teams. Activity planning is siloed and often it is completed with the intention of failure on the pretext that there will be last-minute changes that we have little control over and then we must expedite. The supply chain planner's role integrates the Activity

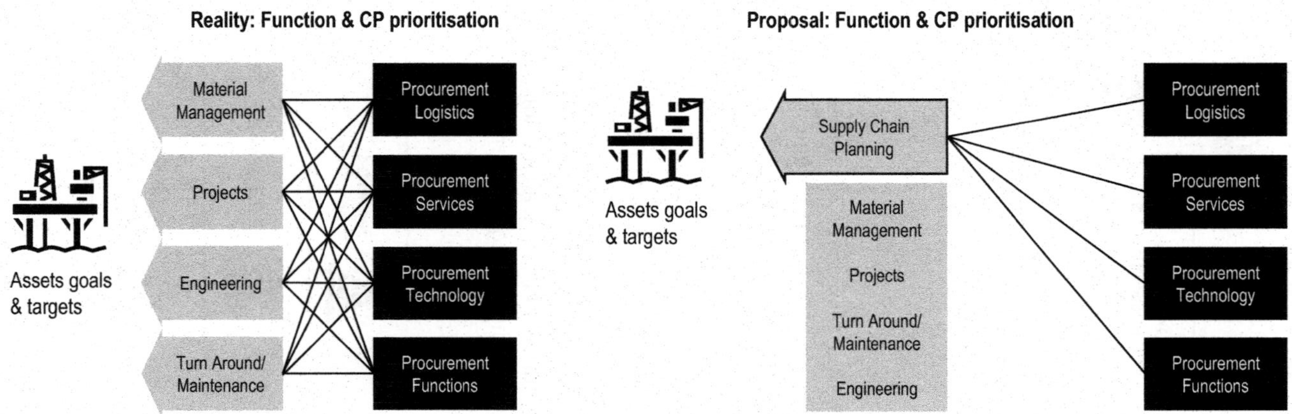

Fig. 5.3 A spaghetti of demand vs. a single point of consolidation

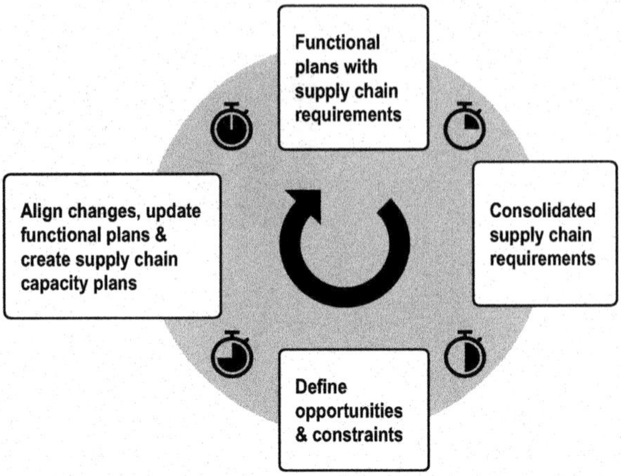

Fig. 5.4 Creating a single version of demand across functions

Planning and related demand plan across the functions to create a single unified view of a Demand Plan across the operating unit.

3. Together with functional planning leads agree on planning items and the associated horizon. Agree on the threshold within which changes are counterproductive and make visible the cost of change.
4. Develop a combined capacity plan and thus the supply chain assurance of material and services delivered over the agreed period. This will need to be updated on a regular period.

This process is illustrated in Fig. 5.5 and in its first attempt takes some effort, but will ultimately prove its worth, as it takes out all the noise and source of variations in the supply chain. Besides, all the subsequent iterations will become much more exception driven.

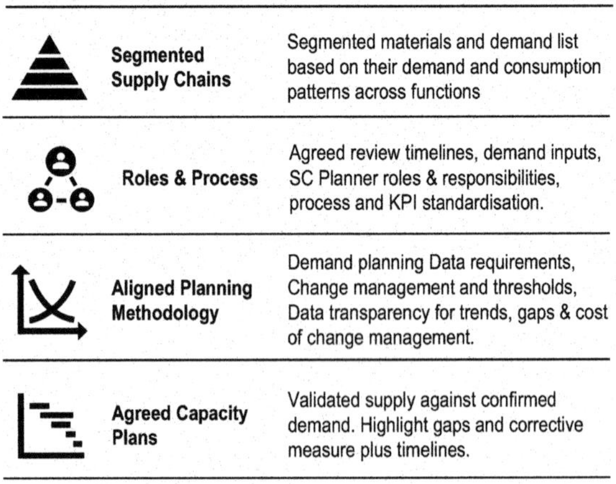

Fig. 5.5 The four outcomes of integrated demand and capacity planning

The most frequent question asked was what is a capacity plan? The best way to demystify this is that it is not a single capacity plan and can possibly take many different forms, depending on the role of the function. So, for instance, where there is a limited resource (aircraft, fleet or warehouse space) this can be directly translated into a 'does it fit' capacity plan and if it does not fit, what do we need to do to increase capacity? On the other hand, where we need continuous and regular delivery of materials such as fuels or chemicals, the capacity planning approach requires a change in the relationship with the vendors, they need the capacity to deliver what is needed when it is needed and therefore, they also need to be capable of being flexible. A third example of capacity planning is whether there is capacity within the contracts, is there sufficient time, coverage and finance to complete the work as intended.

Capacity Planning

It is important to understand where capacity planning sits in the overall planning process. Many businesses drive plans based on the business needs and then ensure the contracts are in place to deliver them. However, it is important to ensure that the plan is also viewed and adjusted in light of the prevailing market conditions and tracked through execution to track performance of the plan (Fig. 5.6). As an output, the capacity plan will look similar to an S&OP plan (Fig. 5.7). The difference being that for a given registered demand, we need to capture the contract coverage for procurement. Starting from the earliest time frame and extending up to the planning horizon, we ensure that contracts are ready for procurement, they have sufficient value, they do not expire halfway or are about to expire. Once we have created this view it can be presented along the axis of Projects, Disciplines and an asset or a group of assets (Figs. 5.8 and 5.9).

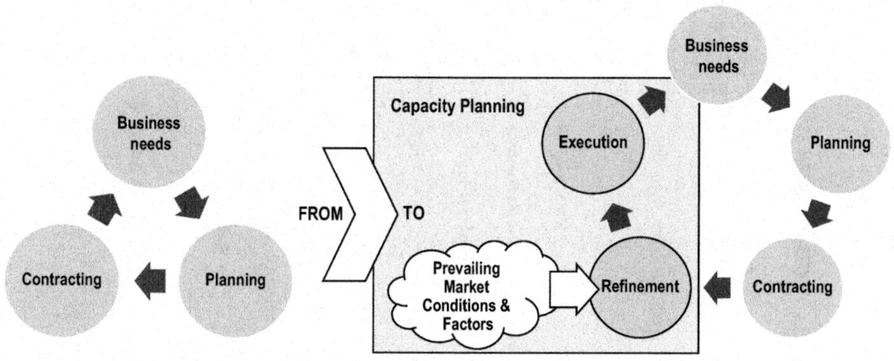

Fig. 5.6 Demystifying capacity planning

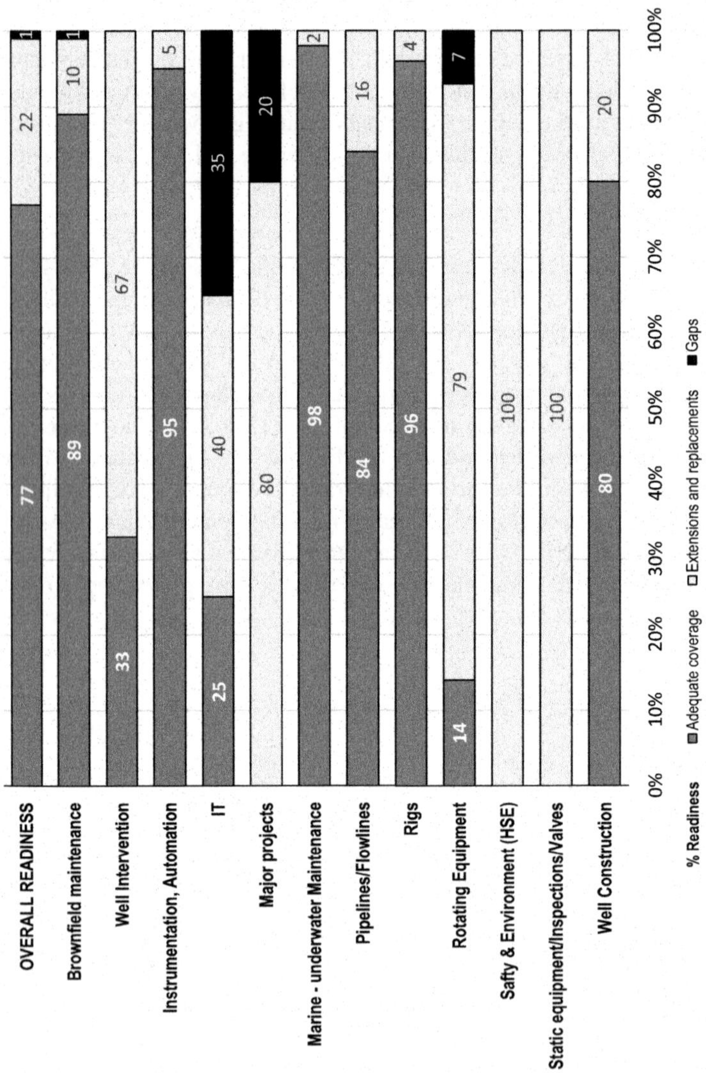

Fig. 5.7 Category demand and associated procurement readiness

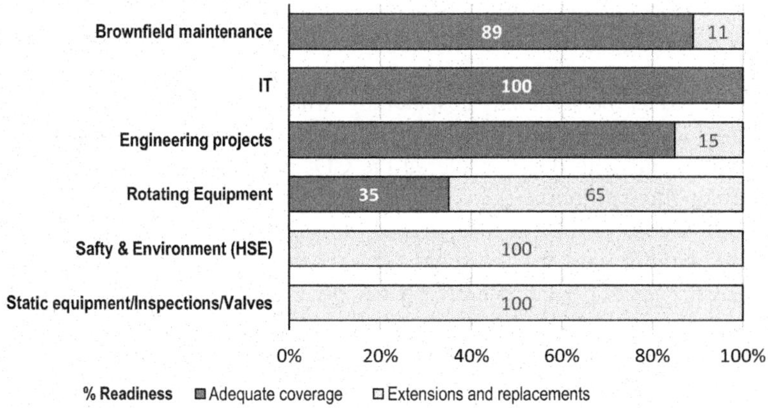

Fig. 5.8 Readiness by functions

5.1.3 *Delivery Schedules: Fix the Basics*

In order to attribute costs to the producing assets, all logistics costs are typically paid for directly by those assets. As such this means that the individual producing assets will target their own optimisation with little or no consideration of optimising the costs across the company. An example of this is an asset that requires material and sends a pickup truck or other small vehicle to collect it from the warehouse.

There are many consequences of this action:

- Suboptimal vehicle utilisation, since nearby assets will also be doing the same.
- Overall high demand for small vehicles.
- No advantage taken from the economy of scale—why not use an articulated truck rather than smaller vehicles.

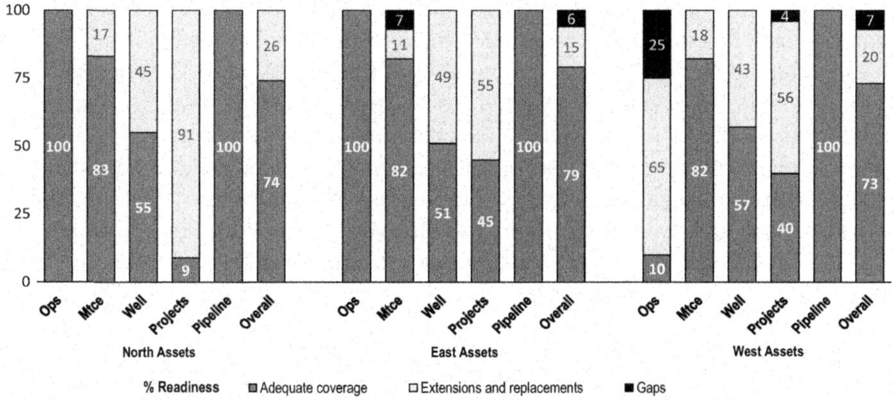

Fig. 5.9 Readiness by a group of assets

- Increased HSSE exposure for both personnel and equipment due to the additional distance travelled by road, which is further increased in areas where escorts are required.
- Uncontrolled demand at the despatching warehouse drives inefficient use of personnel and equipment since peaks are high and troughs are frequent.
- Up until recently, no one considered the CO_2 emissions perspective of running multiple inefficient journeys.
- Although on the surface this might seem like JIT, it is in reality capacity that is kept on standby with the attendant costs. True JIT requires a good degree of planning to get the balance between resource demand and availability. In this instance, the resource availability is effectively not a constraint and therefore the benefits of JIT are wasted through increased inventory storage/maintenance/financing costs.

Similar issues apply across all modes of transport (marine, land and aviation) and by simply focussing on these areas specifically, significant optimisation can be achieved.

In the vessel space, each region had a good justification for all of the vessels required (again driven by the asset requirement rather than the corporate need). This resulted in the inevitable over capacity. Through diligent focus and attention in this space combined with a central planning function, the team was able to identify and remove c100 vessels from the organisation. The service was not impacted but cost and complexity were significantly reduced. This was underpinned by a strict process for approval to step out of the agreed fleet size.

In the aviation space, the approach was different primarily due to the limitation in the availability of helicopters from the vendor. This limitation resulted in the need to re-examine the utilisation and planning of the movement of personnel by helicopter. Although utilisation was high, the measurement was based upon the number of seats PAID for rather than the number of seats actually carrying a passenger. Once these two issues were resolved, the lack of resources was overcome by working smarter rather than securing helicopters from elsewhere.

From a road perspective, the solution was to implement the concept of a milk run that was on both a regular and scheduled basis. Although this concept is not new in many sectors, it required a change in mindset of the organisation. The concept itself is fairly simple (fixed schedule, variable load), but because the 'power' of accountability was moved from the assets to the central team, it was not an easy transition. Once in place, however, the end user (asset) really understood the benefits they gained in terms of regularity of supply as well as the spare capacity that they could use to expand the scope, e.g. returns to the warehouse/workshop, collection of refurbished materials from the workshop etc. Further work here could be done to incorporate all returns including waste and scrap materials, thereby really utilising this return leg capacity.

All of these initiatives resulted in a reduction of fleet, reduced greenhouse gas emission, reduced HSSE exposure, simplification, regular scheduling and ultimately reduced overall OPEX. In the end the trust in the supply chain also increased.

5.1.4 Fix the Internal Decoupling Point

The oil and gas material distribution network typically is not simple and essentially consists of two broad types of material stores, those centrally and those held locally. In principle, this is very similar to the retailing network where there is often a central network, to allow for a diverse range of items to be kept and a local backroom in store where items are kept to fulfill customer demand.

Within the O&G industry, the central stores are typically called supply bases, whose role is to keep the range of materials, which may extend from a rubber washer through to a 20 tonne 40″ valve or a 12 m length of concrete coated pipe. Typically, these materials will be transferred to the asset either by road or water (large vessel, barge etc.). The characteristics of the supply base are that there are good transportation links, the stock is accurate, visible and *relevant.*

The second level of inventory store is the one held locally at the asset, normally at the large producing assets. The characteristics of this type of store are that it is close to the point of use, the stock is accurate, visible and *critical.*

There is a third type of store, affectionately known in some circles as Squirrel Stores. These are essentially very small versions of the local stores, even to the point where they could exist in a cupboard or a drawer and typically exist because of a legacy or a trust issue where local maintenance staff have decided they will keep their own 'spares' to ensure they never 'run out'. The characteristics of these stores are that they are small, the stock is unknown by most, invisible to anyone beyond the people who ordered it and uncontrolled. It is important that these types of stores are removed, as they can be considered at best as simple overstocks or at worst, they are write-offs waiting to happen. In one situation observed, a squirrel store had been created to house rubber belts, undoubtedly, to make sure they were always on hand. However, they had been there so long that they were all out of date and unusable.

Considering the two main types of stores (Central and Local), they are essentially decoupling points and, in our experience, these are set up with the right intent, however, rarely executed well. For instance, in a recent visit to an asset, an unidentifiable item was spotted on the shelf (Fig. 5.10). After investigation, it turned out to be a rubber thimble (for protecting fingers) and two questions were asked:

- Why was this item in stock, since there was no one who could conceivably need a thimble?
- How long had it been there as it had melted into the bottom of the box!

Getting the Right Supply Chain

With the network as complex as it is, the first important step is to appreciate and understand what the potential paths material can take to travel from a vendor through to the end users. There are four different routes as shown in Fig. 5.11.

The first supply chain holds inventory in both the central and the local stores and satisfies the need of having inventory to support the operation through a breadth of material items (central) and having materials close to the point of use (local).

Fig. 5.10 A pulp of forgotten safety equipment

However, this supply chain needs constant management, adjusting what needs to be stored where and how much, as space is often very limited at the asset. It should be used carefully and constantly monitored moving material to the second supply chain as soon as materials become less critical, or space is required for materials with a higher priority. Too often this supply chain is neglected, and significant levels of obsolete material take up critical space at the asset.

The second supply chain has a central storage location which still allows for a significant range of materials to be held in the country but without the additional decoupling point at the asset. This supply chain needs less material management

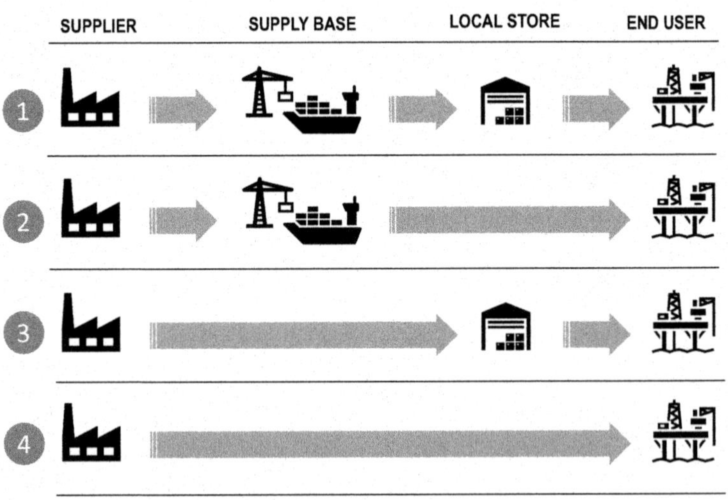

Fig. 5.11 The four supply paths for materials

resources than the first, but since the distance from the asset is further, it is less able to respond to critical emergencies at the asset.

The third supply chain delivers directly from the supplier to the local warehouse and whilst it takes out the largest storage location (and therefore the associated working capital) it is reliant on two specific points, firstly that the vendor has security of supply of the material and secondly that the vendor has the capability to deliver directly to the asset, which may be inaccessible (offshore or in the swamps). This is really only suitable for a few specific items, large bulk items or fuels etc.

The fourth supply chain is also a direct to asset one and although it sounds similar to the third supply chain is typically done via the central and local warehouses, although the material does not appear in inventory at either of these sites. This route requires great planning and more management of the 'in to' country supply chain. It should be used for well-planned activities where demand and requirement times are known well in advance.

5.1.5 Fix the External Decoupling Point

> There is a central difference between the old and new economies: the old industrial economy was driven by **economies of scale**; the new information economy is driven by the economics of networks ... (*Carl Shapiro,* Haas School of Business at the University of California, Berkeley).

The oil and gas industry has long worked on the principle of driving costs down through leveraging the incredible economies of scale available to them. However, as Carl Shapiro points out we need to move away from economies of scale to the economics of networks. This industry has many resources to hand but is unable (or unwilling) to make them accessible to each other. The major issue is one of standardised equipment specifications which precludes inventory sharing across companies or globally across the same company. Holding inventory centrally in a country would enable significant opportunities and benefits to the industry beyond that of simple economies of scale, with all operators drawing from this central point. Where there are insufficient operators in a country to do this, it would even be possible to have hubs of shared inventory held in other countries. This would not be an easy solution to put in place but would help to drive the global inventory levels down. The potential benefit of this approach is shown in Fig. 5.12.

The oil and gas sector is typically built up of Joint Ventures (JVs) since there is a large level of investment required to create the entity in the beginning. It is quite common for the JV to appoint a lead operator, often the partner with the largest share of the business, although where there are two equal partners a JV operating company may be formed. The operating company will have an agreement in place with the co-venturers detailing how they should operate, often with mandated processes and

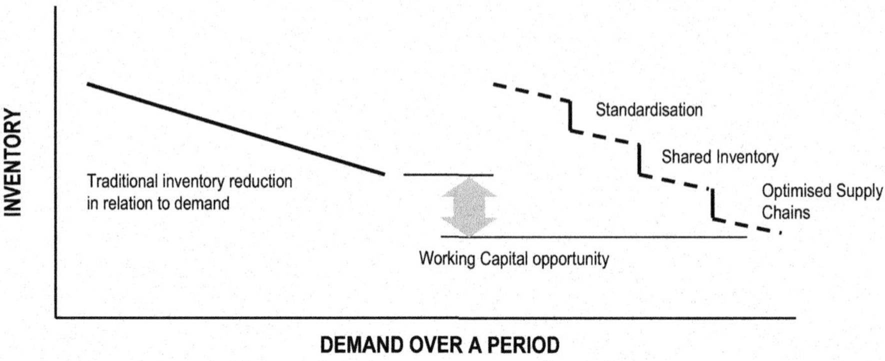

Fig. 5.12 The demand and inventory relationship

practices they need to follow, including the accountability for cost in the event of failure. As such, there is little incentivisation for sharing of inventory across JVs as the operating company may be exposed if failure is caused by the use of it. The operating company will often protect itself by ensuring new material is procured to safeguard this issue. This single point of accountability works against the sharing of inventory across the industry and drives increased waste into the supply chain. In essence, the operator is accountable for procuring inventory and inventory levels and the other partners simply pay their contribution.

This can cause many challenges, specifically around whether the operator really needed the inventory in the first place and then whether the partners are willing to pay or indeed when they pay for it, either at the point of purchase or at the point of consumption. This can be an even bigger issue when the inventory is deemed to be obsolete, and the partners are required to write off this working capital.

Since the operator tends to be the senior partners in the JV they bring their own unique ways of working which may not necessarily include learning from or freely sharing good practice.

Typical industry standards (or rules of thumb) do not exist in the supply chain in the O&G sector like they do in other sectors such as Automotive, FMCG and Healthcare. Internally technical performance standards exist, however even in this space there is a lack of standardisation as each Oil major may (and do) define their own specifications and standards.

The challenge deepens even further as some of the companies may have different standards even within their *own* organisation. This is a result of some very smart and innovative engineers trying to solve a standard problem in a new and unique fashion. Else what is their value add? Cut and paste is not necessarily the most exciting solution to a given problem even though in most cases it is the most cost effective.

The 1970s oil crises put many automotive majors in difficult situations where they had to manage costs more effectively or die. Their response to the challenge was twofold: the first was standardisation which laid the foundation for quality and reliability; the second big change was 'repeatability', which in turn drove consistency. The ability to duplicate modular non-visible parts of the vehicle. Some examples of this include the chassis of VW Sharon, Seat Alhambra and the Ford Galaxy all being made on the same production line because of their shared modular components. The difference was in the trims, engines and visible to the consumer features. The Oil and Gas sector is only talking about this approach five decades later following the 'Lower forever' scenarios.

To fund the new energies, they have to wring everything out of the old energies. Therefore, it is critical they look under every stone to find these savings and if they do not, then they risk premature demise before the new energies take off.

What is stopping these companies from looking under every stone for savings?

- There is no real incentive to do it—inventory is a small cost compared to the value from daily production.
- The oil companies are too inward looking believing they know best.
- By changing the name of the function or expanding the scope of one they believe they have the necessary supply chain expertise, rather than bringing in truly experienced professionals from other industries recognised for their excellence.
- There is no industry pull.
- Little value is attached to the supply chain contribution to the USP of the company.

The NCS (Norwegian Continental Shelf) Sharing Economy program was initiated in late 2016 based on agreement between operators in the Norwegian Oil and Gas Operations Executive Committee to elaborate areas for collaboration to maximise value and strengthen the competitiveness of the Norwegian Continental Shelf. Actors in the industry acknowledged a common responsibility to *maximise* the profitability of production from the shelf. The project started in early 2017 under the name Market Place project and has now developed into a program called NCS Sharing Economy. You can learn more about it by visiting their site at www.virtualinventory.no.

What could the future look like:

Activity	Benefit
Standardise specifications across the industry	Ability to share inventory between companies Less time to create bespoke specifications
Hold inventory across the sector	In country common stocking points reducing working capital inventory and OPEX Lower HSSE exposure due to fewer stocking points Industry-wide availability driving cooperation
Focus on optimising supply chains for the good of all	Delivering lower GHG emissions Sharing equipment Being more resilient

5.1.6 Segment the Inventory and Procurement Plans

In module 4, we discussed the physical supply chain, i.e. how we manage the physical flow of materials through the network. We discussed how it is essential to manage the materials depending on a number of business factors, that is how critical they are to the running of the operation and whether they are used for planned or corrective maintenance. The business has moved from one supply chain to fit all where the default was to stock (safest) as much as possible to the deployment of the supermarket model creating the four supply processes, but this in itself is not entirely world class and further fine tuning is required.

Across other industries, there is a granularity of segmentation that goes to the next level where the specific characteristics of the product drive a different way of handling it through the supply chain. Take for example the food retailing business. Fresh food is handled in a very different way to ambient goods as mentioned earlier, it is managed in a stockless way, clearing the decks at the end of every day whereas ambient goods are traditionally stocked items. Even here, the stocked items have been further subdivided into super-fast moving items, managed in display units (dollies, half pallets etc.) which are managed much more like a just-in-time product. This enables the business to hold little inventory (if any at all) whilst minimising the handling effort through the supply by having supply chain handling units that also double up as display units. The fashion industry shows another way of effectively managing products depending on where they are in their life cycle, at launch they are delivered in single launch packs containing different sizes and colours to make it easy to merchandise, but thereafter treating each size and colour as a single SKU and replenished accordingly. These types of refinements have been in existence for many years, but similar principles have not been adopted in the oil and gas sector.

The very blunt instruments used in oil and gas deprive the business from fine tuning, although there have been attempts to implement it. For instance, one such system we came across tried to fine-tune the replenishment levels at an SKU level through quite sophisticated data and trend analysis. However, the ambition was too great since it was targeted at a level of detail that never asked some basic questions—did this material need to be in inventory in the first place? did it need to be in all warehouses? etc. A better approach considered the criticality of the equipment based on performance history and therefore whether the associated spares should be held locally, centrally or ordered as required. This type of segmentation ensured a robust and cost-efficient segmentation strategy. When you plan a trip, it is essential that you prepare properly, know where you are going, decide the route to be taken, prepare the car, make sure there is enough fuel etc. You cannot simply expect to get to the destination if all the basics are not in place first.

Segmentation is a prerequisite to deciding whether to procure to order (PTO) or procure to inventory (PTI), these decisions in turn should drive the contracting strategy (Fig. 5.13). The current approach is that the contracting strategy drives procurement which in turn drives the level of inventory, the supply chain has a

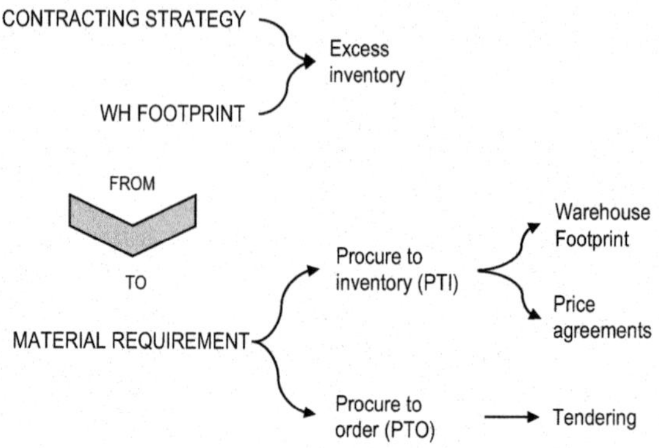

Fig. 5.13 Material requirements and contracting strategy

FOCUS on COST. However, it is important to use the wisdom used in other industries (FMCG, Fashion etc.) to segment the materials first, which in turn drives the contracting strategy and ultimately delivery and this changes the supply chain to have a FOCUS on DEMAND. This way of working moves the organisation from having to deal with problems when they occur with excess inventory, high costs or poor availability to a situation where the characteristics of the product itself (via segmentation) determine the contracting strategy and therefore this lowers the risk of issues after procurement.

The focus on cost has its origins in project design, where the overall cost of the project and the time to deliver is much more important than the impact on the 'run and maintain' phase. Since little consideration is given to 'run and maintain', what looks like a good deal at the project phase can impact the operation for the rest of its life cycle. Figure 5.14 shows how segmentation should work and a rigorous adoption of these rules enables the business to clearly see which category material falls into and therefore what course of action should be taken to procure them.

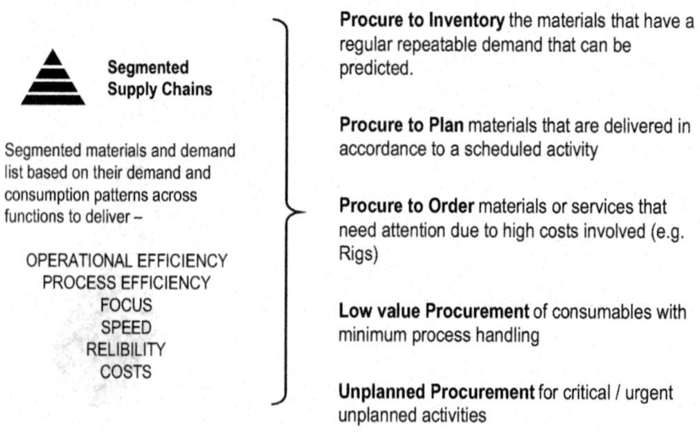

Fig. 5.14 Supply chain segmentation

5.1.7 *Control the Inbound Supply Chains*

The easiest way of receiving materials into the country is to have them delivered to the point of internal distribution, i.e. delivered duty paid (DDP). This way, all the effort of getting it from point of origin, inbound logistics, through customs and at the point of need is contracted out. This approach no doubt again has its origins with engineering, procurement and construction contractors (EPC), where the cradle to grave delivery of a project is outsourced to a third party. DDP is a good way of working, especially in countries where internal experience and resources are limited. However, using DDP does not come without risk, and it has been recognised that the DDP deliveries have in them two inherent weaknesses:

First DDP has an inherent lack of effective compliance control in that it is assumed all regulations and laws are being complied with by the supplier. Unfortunately, this is always open to interpretation and can vary on a case-to-case basis. The Panalpina facilitation payment is a significant example where this lack of visibility and control caused substantial fines to both Panalpina and companies for whom they were working. In a US plea bargain, they agreed to pay $236.5 million in penalties in relation to the payment of customs officials for customs clearance. As part of that investigation, a well-known Oil and Gas company became involved through a subsidiary and, ultimately paid $30 million in criminal penalties in relation to $2 million paid to subcontractors for the purposes of making these payments to the customs officials.

Secondly, the use of DDP incoterms can lead to an inflated cost to bring materials into the country, which can be significant with the importing company adding their mark-up to all aspects of the costs without stating what these base costs are.

Currently, suppliers are measured fundamentally on cost with service, as a requirement, nowhere on the selection criteria. This has a significant impact on the overall supply chain performance since we do not learn nor deal with vendor inadequacies. In many cases, we observed that the same vendor was constantly being awarded contracts because they were the cheapest or they are an approved partner in our framework agreement. This gave rise to the following outcomes:

- Mistakes were repeated at both the enterprise and the country levels.
- The focus was almost always based on cost and not performance.
- The only situation where punitive actions were taken were based on ethics and compliance failures.

In many cases, we have observed that the local teams still have to manage and guide the vendors on customs controls to ensure compliance. This means that companies are effectively paying for this service twice and, there is a risk that compliance is vulnerable at critical points especially in the relationship between individual clearing agents and the customs officials directly. In one instance, over 150 different clearing agents were being used to service one company and the integrity and compliance of all of these companies could not be guaranteed.

This has resulted in an anomaly in the organisational design where the role of an expeditor is not seen as an exception but normalised into everyday activities. An expeditor's role should be to troubleshoot the outliers to progress the issues here. In reality under this scenario, all orders are outliers, therefore all require expediting.

- Step one of the compliance processes was to consolidate this number to less than 10 and ensure all vendors in the country used one of these nominated clearing agents.
- Step two was to move from DDP to FCA (Free Carrier) terms, where the purchasing operator buys the materials and arranges themselves for collection from the producing OEM and arranges for the entire primary logistics leg into the country through a limited number of freight forwarders.

This control of the inbound supply chain has an additional benefit above the compliance and cost, namely that the visibility, control and sequencing of inbound materials are much greater and can be aligned better with the demand within the business. This additional control is not free and requires additional internal resources and capability within the operator supply chain organisation. In conjunction with module 6 (segmentation), we should be much better placed to track supplier performance with this approach, and we should limit expeditors to manage exceptions only and invest the effort into performance managing the vendors to improve their service.

5.1.8 *Promote the Suppliers to Stakeholders: Streamline the Link*

All of the parties involved across the end-to-end supply chain are critical in delivering success, but as important is the type and effectiveness of interface between them. Often suppliers are simply considered as a provider of the required goods or service (and as previously mentioned chosen on the lowest cost option) very rarely are they elevated to the status of partner, with whom problems are shared and solutions arrived at together. The biggest misconception is that since the oil company is a big customer what is needed should be delivered despite late and poor planning, late placement of orders and highly customised specifications.

In reality, the Oil and Gas industry is important to many OEMs but not necessarily critical to their overall business success and therefore are lower in priority than some other sectors (e.g. power generation). To achieve agility in the capacity plan it is essential that the OEMs are front and centre in the planning process so that they can establish a f[illegible]ion plan that can be modified as time moves on. The motor and aviation i[illegible] have refined this process considerably over many years such that it is diffi[illegible]inguish between where the manufacturer plan starts and the OEMs plan [illegible] it is just one seamless continuous plan. In IOCs, this is not a common [illegible], although it does happen in project planning and execution, but rarely h[illegible]n the run and maintain side of the business.

In [illegible] to the integration with suppliers, the pan industry integration yields an even gre[illegible] opportunity for instance Pettersen in Norway/UK/Nam coordinates fleet

requirements across the Oil and Gas sector. This does, however, often take a significant and driven intervention from external parties (e.g. government) to facilitate and encourage this alignment across the companies to achieve specification alignment and complementary processes. Examples of this are that in Norway there is a drive to hold common inventory across the industry in order to reduce costs and in Nigeria the OPTS organisation (Oil Producers Trade Section) has a specific program to share both inventory and logistics resources also to reduce costs.

The stronger the influence of these external parties the quicker and more complete the solution that is driven. Where the industry is left to deal with these issues by itself, they often fail due to their perceived internal difference which no party is prepared to change which has been seen in the United Kingdom where inventory shares seem to be too difficult to achieve.

In West Africa, we have seen that in one of the ports, 4 IOCs have independent inventory storage locations. Roughly each of the IOCs has inventory to the value of c$250 m, which means that overall, along the length of the facility, these inventories total upward of $1 bn. There is a good chance that much of the inventory is repeated across these IOCs and, although the specifications vary, it would be possible through inventory integration and sharing to reduce this overall by two-thirds. This has certainly not been the attention of these companies. As discussed previously, there is a significant role for the government or pan industry bodies to drive this type of inventory sharing. Without this stimulus, the general attitude from the individual companies is that they have sufficient inventory so why bother.

The government plays a pivotal role in driving this level of integration and may need to resort to legislation as a means to achieving compliance[1] with it. Simply having well-intentioned bodies is not sufficient to achieve the required outcome. Without legislation, the oil companies view these initiatives as an interesting, but diversionary, opportunity that takes too much effort and too long to deliver any payback. The Government must be involved to look at the long-term viability of this industry rather than taking short-term 'get rich quick' decisions.

Do the right thing vs doing the thing right. The answer to this dilemma often lies in the type of approach to an issue an industry has, is it a response to an immediate need or is it a strategic decision, to do the thing right vs to do the right thing. As an example of this, you can look at the difference between safety in the motor trade and safety in the oil and gas industry. In order to understand the difference, it is important to establish the origin of the decisions. Oil and gas companies have had significant and major safety incidents, for example Deep Water Horizon in the Gulf of Mexico and Piper Alpha in the North Sea. These tragedies resulted in multiple losses of life and significant financial penalties, but it drove stricter cultures of safety in these organisations and an attitude 'of doing the thing right'.

Looking across to the car industry, however, there are a number of examples of philanthropic actions taken by industries to improve the overall standards for that

[1] In many places, with local content requirements, an additional level of complexity is introduced by needing to buy goods and services from an indigenous vendor, who in turn purchases them from the OEM. It is therefore critical that the extended nature of these relationships is appreciated and incorporated into any Supply Chain development plan, or these will result in inflexibility.

industry. For instance, the invention of the three-point seat belt by Nils Bohlin at Volvo, which was shared across the industry to become the industry standard. Tesla is on the verge of sharing their electric vehicle technology, which could become the standard in this area for the future. These sorts of actions drive an industry forward and demonstrate an approach of 'doing the right thing'.

It is therefore critical that vendors and OEMs are included as part of the definition of the solution rather than simply being viewed as a service provider. In this way, they will be part of the solution, know the goal and understand the flexibility required in the delivery plan.

5.1.9 Know Your Vulnerabilities

Nearly all businesses have defined business continuity plans, which focus on what to do if any one of a number of events happen, for instance, if a particular warehouse is unable to operate due to industrial action or fire. These events are often short term in their nature although the more serious occurrences (e.g. fire) might have a longer-term impact. These are reactive, near-term solutions to unplanned events.

However, one of the lessons learned from COVID-19 was that there are global events that have far-reaching impacts on an organisation for which the business continuity plan is not able to cope adequately. We quickly came to realise that although these plans were necessary, they were not sufficient to manage these prolonged and multifaceted events, impacting different countries, sectors and businesses all of whom had some dependency on each other. Many sectors were unprepared for this situation (PPE, medical etc.) and this included O&G.

So, what to do? Is it sufficient to assume that this type of situation will not happen again? Or that everyone will take the lessons learned and make their supply chains much more resilient? No, it certainly is not the right approach. It was identified early on that there could be hidden vulnerabilities, some so small that in themsėlves they seem insignificant, but if they occur, it could have a devastating impact. Think for an instance where the manufacturer of pipeline clamps can no longer supply these items because their raw material supplier has a problem. So despite the tier 1 supplier being ok, the non-availability of critical repair material results in leaks not being able to be repaired.

To combat this, we developed a more holistic approach of looking at the supply chain vulnerability to:

1. Establish significant potential risk scenarios (at a country level and specific to it) (Fig. 5.15).
2. Test the resilience of existing plans against these scenarios to highlight the weaknesses (Fig. 5.16).
3. Conduct a deep dive analysis on the most vulnerable of these areas (Fig. 5.17).
4. Create a mitigation plan for these risks, where some of the mitigations may only be triggered in a specific situation (Fig. 5.18).
5. Monitor and react to the plan on a regular basis.

Step 1—Create potential scenarios

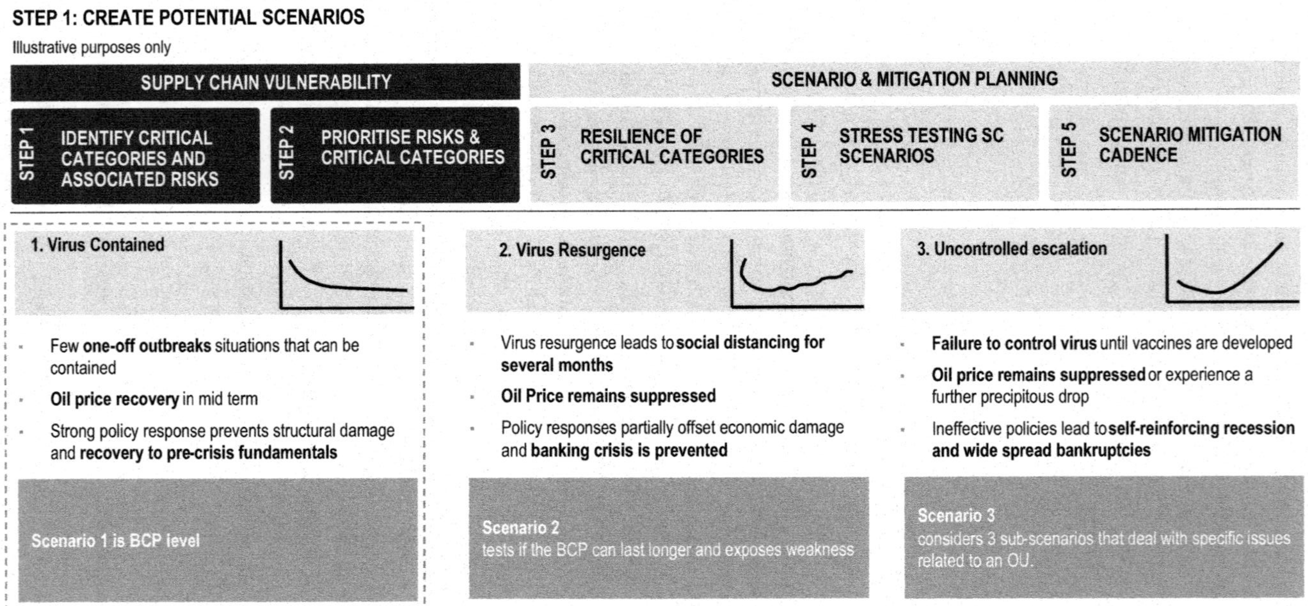

Fig. 5.15 A structured approach to vulnerability

Step 2—High-level review of resilience (30, 60, 90 days) to identify potential weak spots

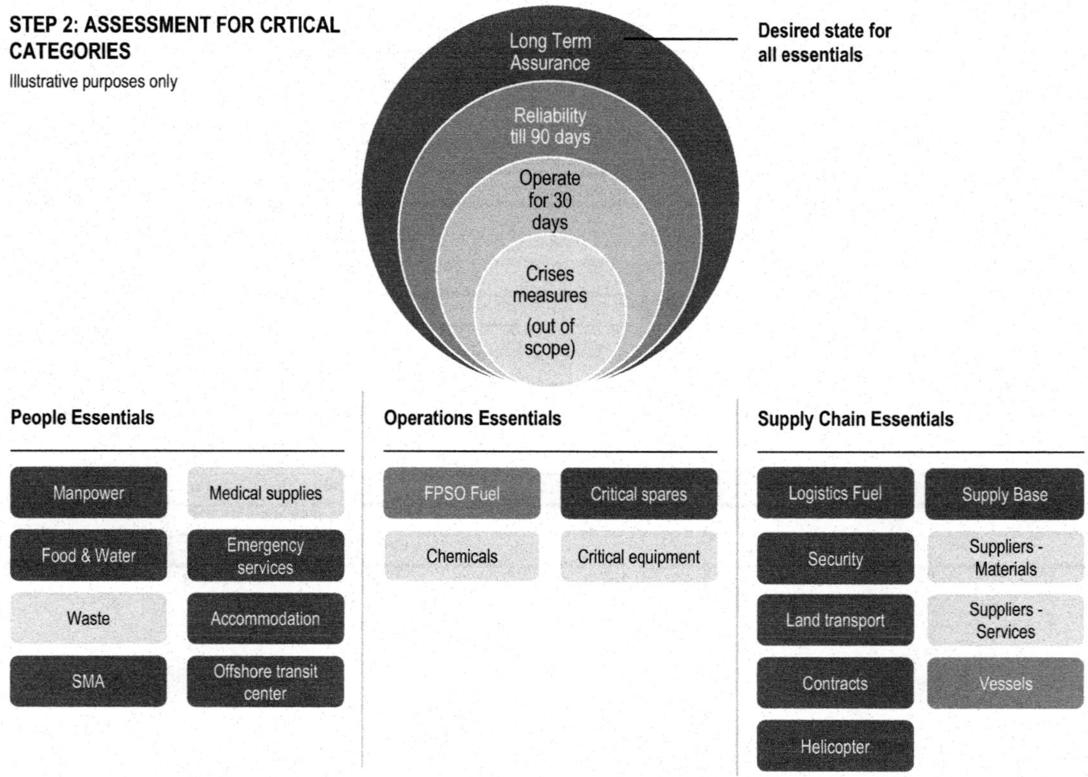

Fig. 5.16 Looking beyond the 90 days

Step 3—Deep dive into risk areas

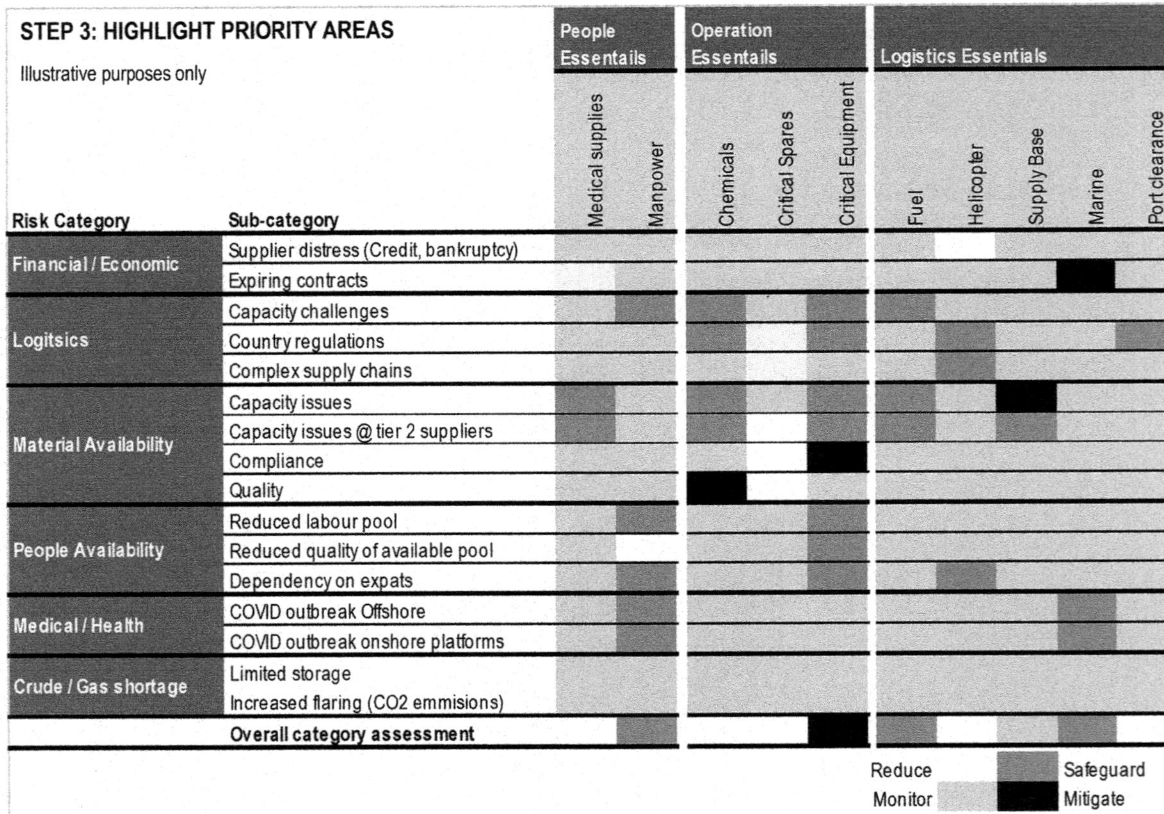

Fig. 5.17 The risk quilt

Step 4—Mitigation plan

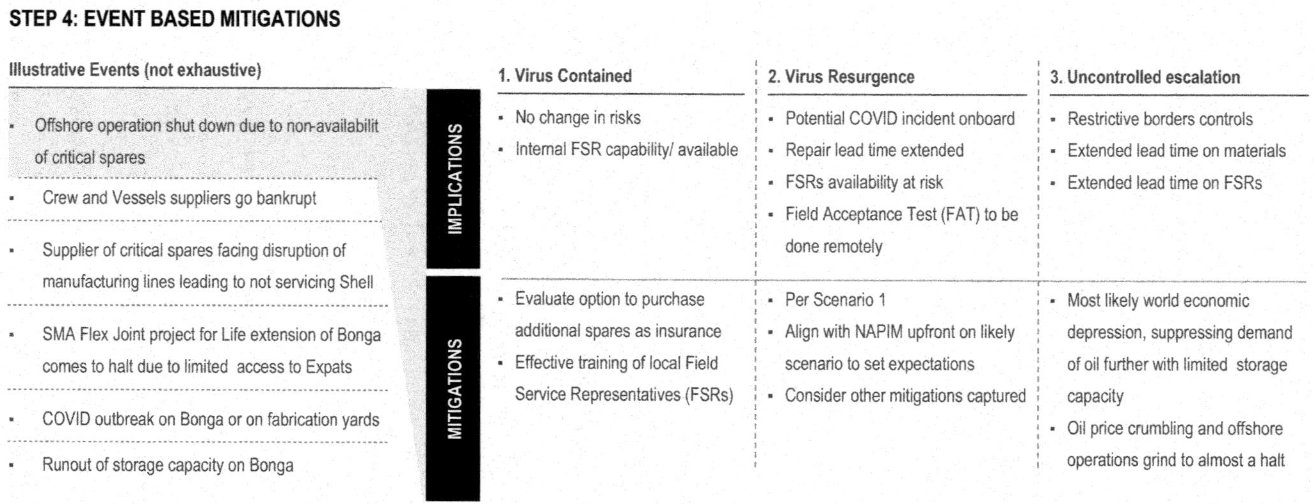

Fig. 5.18 Planning mitigations

Step 5—Monitor regularly

Regularly connect with the team to assess progress, to ensure the risks identified previously have now been either eliminated or mitigated. Followed by identification of new risks to review.

This management of vulnerabilities is an enhanced version of the BCP at a county level, which by design is more proactive in nature. There are actions that can be taken in advance of a potential event occurring to ensure the supply chain is more resilient if that event should happen (for instance, having alternative suppliers on different continents). These vulnerabilities should also be completed at an enterprise level. This was a revelation to the industry.

At a contracting level, the approach is typically rudimentary in that if the service/material is critical then multiple vendors are engaged. The due diligence on the stability of tier two suppliers, i.e. where they are drawing their resources from, is rarely considered in terms of the overall vulnerability of the category. We saw evidence that it was only the local resilience that was considered rather than global resilience.

One of the examples we came across was the supply of chemicals, which are supplied in concentrate form from the USA, Europe or China and then diluted in-country. The risks in this area were more extensive than most people appreciated:

- Lockdown in one or more supply countries would impact cost and lead time.
- Lack of available freight from specific countries.
- Limited alternative suppliers from other countries.
- Local outbreak of COVID preventing dilution.

  No account was made for these risks, the award for supply was based on cost alone rather than security of supply as well as cost.

The oil and gas industry should run this type of assessment on an ongoing basis in order to be confident of their supply chain abilities in the long term. All contract awards, all vendor assessments and all tier two suppliers should be assessed, potentially extending this to include where they get their resources from, as part of the standard operating methodology.

5.1.10 You Can Only Manage What You See

In the same way that end-to-end planning is critical when optimising a supply chain, it is also essential to have end-to-end visibility of the physical flow of materials across the supply chain.

Depending on where in the world the asset is located will determine the length and complexity of the supply chains. For instance, if the asset is based in the USA or Europe, suppliers are often close to hand or at least within the same continent. In addition, the systems deployed by these suppliers are typically modern and have the capability to be digitally linked together. In this way, it is possible to get end-to-end visibility of the physical supply chain relatively easily.

However, there are many Oil and Gas rich areas where the physical supply chains are both long and complex including examples such as Africa, India and Kazakhstan. Not only are there insufficient suppliers located in the country, but the demands of the government require that a significant local content component is achieved, with the intention of driving local development and future sustainability. In an ideal world, this would have both a positive impact on the development of the country and would gradually, over time, enable the industry to stand on its own feet. Rarely does this happen? Often what results is an intermediary who is simply a briefcase company, one through which the order is placed, but has little interest in anything except the fee for handling the transaction.

The result? A complex supply chain with an additional transactional vendor between the oil and gas company and the OEM. A vendor who does not have much (if any) systems capability, who slows down the process and prevents visibility through the supply chain. Couple this with a similar approach with freight forwarders and there are significant gaps throughout the chain, where material may disappear for months, even years.

This combination of complexity and visibility gaps drives businesses to attempt to protect themselves through other means, employing expeditors for instance whose only role is to chase everyone for everything, which is definitely a non-value-adding activity.

In essence, the lack of visibility of the supply chain causes further erosion of trust from the end users. In turn, this lack of trust has an adverse impact on both operating and capital costs of the business and therefore its profitability. The trust issue encourages parts of the business to solve the availability issues themselves, either through ordering more than they require or ordering through inefficient channels, for example ordering material as part of a service, where costs can be significantly inflated, rather than procuring through a material purchase order.

The introduction of an end-to-end visibility tool can deliver significant benefits to the business, regardless of its location in the world. In an area where vendors have a high level of digitisation and short supply chains, end-to-end visibility can quickly identify where issues appear and drive rapid decisions based on relevant up-to-date facts. In countries with less developed digitisation, whilst it requires manual updates by the various parties, it enables easy identification of exceptions and directs the resource and time to the problem areas rather than having to treat all procurement orders as potential issues. The second solution, although not as robust as the first solution, will enable time to be freed up to drive an overall better outcome.

Visibility needs to be looked at through a number of different lenses starting with the short term operational visibility, where efficient resource allocation occurs, through medium-term visibility for capacity planning, all the way to long-term business planning (Fig. 5.19). The benefits of this approach are shown in Fig. 5.20.

In an MRO supply Chain, the maintenance strategies used are a major part of defining its characteristics. Essentially there are two types of maintenance strategy, schedule maintenance or run to failure. In a low oil price environment, there is the

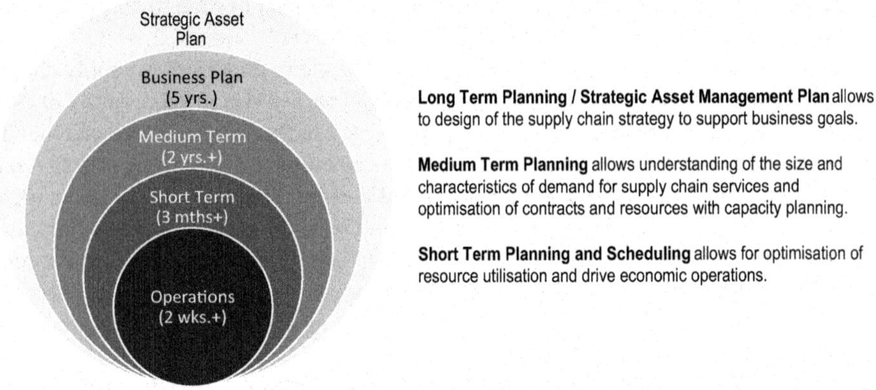

Fig. 5.19 Driving demand visibility

temptation to move from a scheduled maintenance approach to a run to failure one in order to save costs. However, this will only save cost in the short term, but it has an even more detrimental effect on demand variability. Variability is a concept that is not commonly understood in Oil and Gas. Where a system has an $n + 1$ design (i.e. there is excess capacity, for example where there is one more compressor than is actually needed Ref Fig. 3.4) theoretically a run to failure strategy can work, so if there is a breakdown on one piece of equipment the spare is used. However, what happens in real life is that the business is gambling on running to fail against two

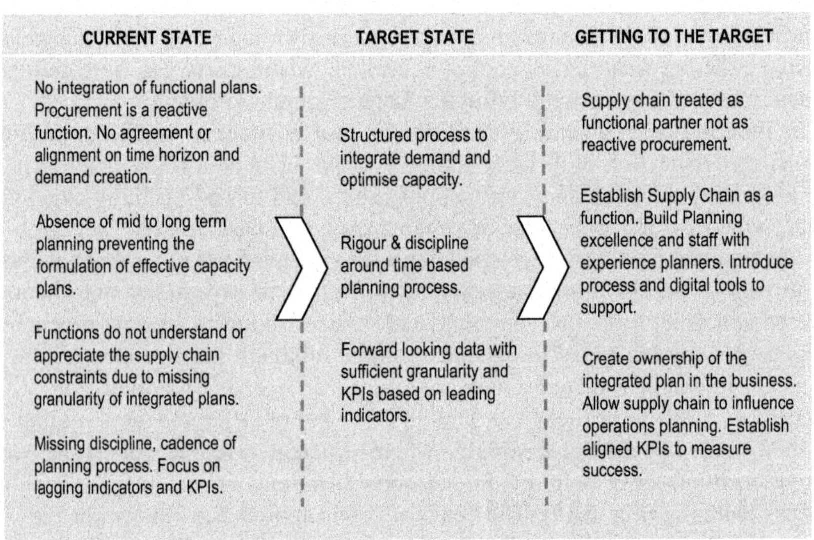

Fig. 5.20 Getting to the target state

machines and there is a significant risk, which we have frequently seen, that when failure occurs and you need to swap over at the time needed, the spare machine is not available. If on the other hand you have an '$n + 0$' design (i.e. no spare capacity), then you cannot run to failure, a corrective maintenance plan must be in place. Therefore, a run to failure strategy is counter intuitive to the supply chain and counterproductive to the business.

In order to drive a reliable and resilient supply chain, it is essential that the operational team keeps on the top of their maintenance schedules and plans. The temptation to allow the 'tail to wag the dog', i.e. to allow financial pressures to drive the maintenance strategy must be avoided at all costs. Deploying a run to failure approach creates a bow wave (or bullwhip effect) of cost in 2–3 years' time when all the production systems reach a critical repair requirement within a very short period.

Many businesses employ a Plan—Do—Review (PDR) approach to problem solving, however, this approach has a fundamental assumption that the original plan itself was good, it was integrated, and it was reviewed properly across functions. In an ideal world it would be better to adopt a Plan—Review—Do—Review process, which allows a full review of the plan (maybe by an independent party) prior to execution. We are not judging the integrity of the time-tested model of PDR in a continuous improvement world, however, in the Oil and Gas sector the plan needs to have gone through its own iterative process before the execution. Simply using PDR is not good enough, if the Plans lack completeness and detail. If the PDR cycle is short, typically on a weekly basis, then the process continuously corrects itself. However, for medium and long-term planning it becomes imperative that we improve the plans through multiple iterations before the execution date to check and recheck the plan.

Management of change (MoC) in the Oil and Gas industry is almost always seen in the context of safety, as this is indeed the most important thing in this industry. Lower priorities are production and finance impact but rarely is any consideration given to Supply Chain impact during MoC.

Historically we failed to plan. Now we have a plan but with failure built in and therefore it comes as no surprise when we fail. In this situation, no one worries about MoC as the failures are per plan. The core issue with this situation is that since we are in a constant failure mode, our norm is one of firefighting not continuous improvement. All related inefficiencies (poor planning, poor availability etc.) are masked by production and oil prices.

A supply chain control tower is designed to execute a plan that is clearly defined to begin with. Whilst it is not designed to change the plan for production, turnaround or project execution delivery, it helps to improve the plan and manage unforeseen risks towards the successful execution of it.

Control Towers are often misrepresented. Any set of visibility KPIs are often deemed to represent a control tower, however, typically the KPIs are lagging and therefore offer little control and are simply reporting mechanisms or dashboards. A true well-defined control tower needs to have the following attributes:

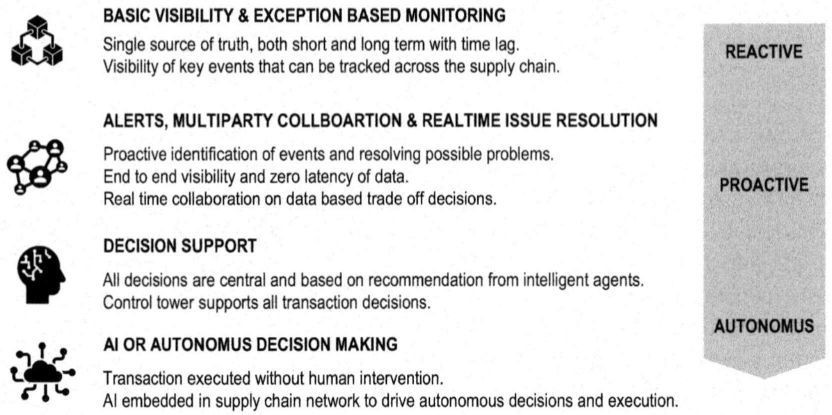

Fig. 5.21 The stages of control tower maturity

1. PLAN: It needs to measure progress against a predetermined plan.
2. KPIs: It must monitor leading KPIs, rather than lagging ones.
3. ACTION: It drives corrective actions that positively influence the outcome.
4. PROCESS: It has a set well-defined process to manage it with expert resources and governance framework.

There are different levels of maturity of a control tower as shown in Fig. 5.21, and it is essential to recognise these levels and have a deliberate plan to move from one level to the next.

Usually, the majority of the end-to-end data for a control tower to exist is already in the system covering the end-to-end process (Fig. 5.22), but they are inaccessible and stored in disparate and disconnected systems. In many instances, there are also legacy systems that do not talk to each other and are owned by departments who

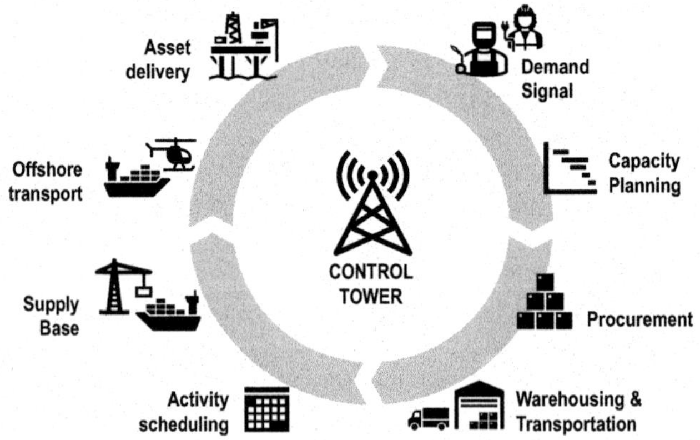

Fig. 5.22 Typical control tower coverage

generally do not talk to each other! This may be a common challenge across most oil and gas assets.

Modern ERP systems offer such end-to-end information functionality, however, from our experience, this is rarely specified and designed from the outset, and therefore becomes a difficult and cost-prohibitive transition at a later stage.

The tried and trusted way of pulling a Control Tower together would be to bring everyone together in your War Room, where visual management, active exchange of information and change in plans will ensure the process flows across the entire supply chain. Co-location of key team members in the operations also helps with this situation. With the combination of virtual teams as well as COVID-19, this type of solution will become less and less feasible and therefore it is critical that these attributes are replicated as closely as possible onto the digital platform.

It is critical that the teams and organisation go on their own journey of discovery. When Tenzing and Hilary first conquered Everest they achieved something that no one believed to be possible. Since then, however, with improved path definition, equipment, weather prediction, advances in medical science to overcome the impact of altitude etc. it is possible for 'tourist climbers' to achieve this feat with a fair amount of certainty despite the risks and challenges. However, for anyone to say they have climbed Everest, they physically need to climb Everest. The same applies to the maturity of Control Tower development. Whilst it might be easier and quicker to progress through steps, you still need to go through all of them.

The manual Control Tower is probably the best way to start this process, especially in large organisations, because it does the following:

- Demonstrates to the organisation the reason for the process working the way it works, since it is manually developed and adjusted to fit the specific environment it is being used in.
- Demonstrates to the leadership how a change in organization and behaviours can deliver benefits.
- Once an autonomous system is created, it should not be seen as an opportunity to de-skill or replace the workforce, instead it should be used as a tool for the smart operators to enhance the results and achieve better execution.
- Enables the principle of working 'smarter and not harder'.
- Drives cost reduction from better interface points, removing duplication and delivering improved service with lower working capital.

It is critical that organisations go through this process from start to finish and that they do not get blindsided by promises of quick fixes delivered by digital tools. If the tools are already in place, an organisation should consider using the digital tools together in a Manual Control Tower room to educate and upskill the organisation in the basics of this principle. The tools themselves are not the solution, they only support the human capacity to extract the maximum from them (Fig. 5.23).

This is about driving leadership behaviours to understand the benefits to be achieved from visual management and to appreciate why it is important to have daily stand-up meetings. It is therefore critical that for a control tower to be effective

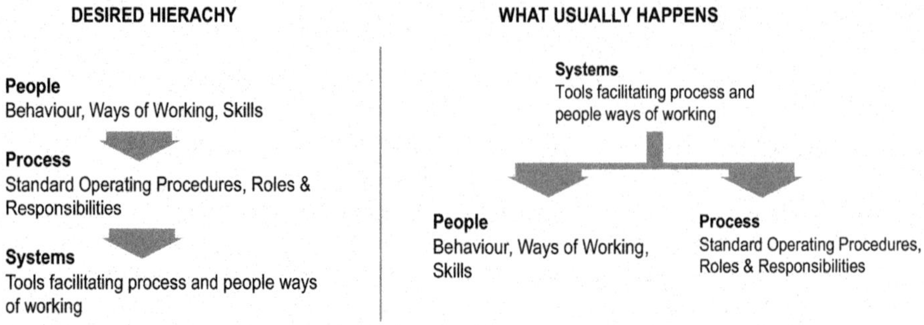

Fig. 5.23 Maturing towards a control tower

it must have the support and fundamental understanding from the leadership, and it must use a standardised set of KPIs.

As an example, for almost 20 years, Tescos used a balanced scorecard, covering Customer, Community, Operations, People and Finance and they deemed it critical to get the balance right between each of these quadrants. In this way, they tracked if they were too focused on one specific area to the detriment of another. Although this was replaced in 2015, it had served its purpose to ensure that the focus across the business covered the major elements.

It is critical for businesses to, first of all, establish what the most important areas of focus should be and then to ensure that KPIs are developed to ensure performance is measured in them and to assess whether the business is going in the right direction.

5.1.11 *Standardise the KPIs*

There are different levels of KPIs that should be driven from the business at the top and to the functions at the bottom. The KPIs at the top are Lagging, showing the performance of the business overall and as they go progressively lower in the organisation, they should progressively become Leading at the bottom, because this is the level that can change and influence the top-level Lagging indicators.

At the top-level, it is about measuring performance and at the bottom it is about holding people accountable to deliver and focussing their attention on the improvement areas. Getting this structure and cascade wrong will render any set of KPIs useless. It is important to understand that 'cascade' does not equate to 'replicate', all too often this is the common misunderstanding that if it is in the business' scorecard then it needs to be in the functions. In truth, the behaviours must change and whatever is in the business scorecard needs to be 'translated' in the functional scorecard by asking the question:

What will this function do specifically to support the business objectives?

That may seem common sense, but we are hardly the first to observe that common sense is often not common!

Let us just for a moment explain a little more about Leading and Lagging indicators. Lagging indicators are effectively the rolled-up result after something has happened, they report historical performance, and they cannot be changed but they are designed to show trends (e.g. sales growth) or comparisons between specific periods (e.g. Profit and Loss statement). Leading indicators on the other hand show what is happening during the process of delivering and they report KPIs that contribute to the final performance and allow corrective actions to be taken to influence the final outcome. An example of a leading indicator could be the length of time it takes to place an order, getting internal approvals and processing to raise a purchase order. If this time starts becoming extended, then it needs to be dealt with immediately in order to ultimately minimise the delays in the time the materials are delivered and therefore the impact on production downtime. Both types of KPIs are critical but it is essential that they are used at the correct level in the organisation.

So how does this relate to the Oil and Gas sector? Well, our observations have shown that we focus on lagging KPIs at all levels through the organisation (Fig. 5.24), so we effectively accept the results for what they are, promising that things will change in the future. We are always looking in the rear-view mirror when we should be looking at the front to chart our path, avoid crashes and drive the business forward.

We are creatures of habit and we have been brought up on lagging indicators, where significantly fluctuating KPIs are the norm and initiative after initiative is deployed to try to get them under control. It is imperative that the leading indicators (in every function) report on Cost, Revenue and Safety and this should not be optional. The entire enterprise mantra is that the business should make money safely.

It is not unknown for senior leaders to shy away from confronting KPIs. A good example we observed was On Time KPI for the procurement function. The On Time % was stubbornly low and therefore almost always avoided by leadership and therefore effectively became a 'soft KPI'. This is a classic example of a cross-functional KPI, i.e. one where many 'fingers' are in the pie. By holding this 'lagging' KPI in the second or third level of Fig. 5.24, it just resulted in a blame game. However, if relevant leading indicators had been used in the functions, it would have driven cross-functional collaboration which would have eventually improved the overall On Time KPI. The leadership should seek out these opportunities for cross-functional engagement and collaborations. The leading indicators need to be relevant and explicit to what each function needs to deliver. The following functional leading KPIs are examples of what should be measured:

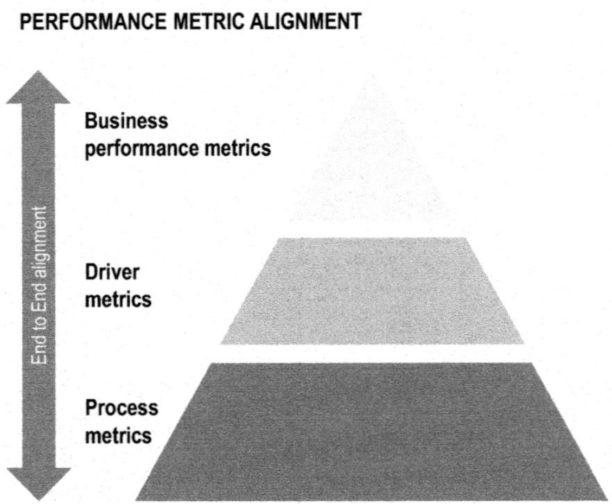

PERFORMANCE METRIC DESCRIPTION

METRIC LEVEL	DESCRIPTION	MEASUREMENT LEVEL	REVIEWD & MANAGED BY
Business Performance Metrics	**Overall business performance**. e.g.. - Production - Safety - Opex reduction - Capex efficiency	- Asset level - Asset extension - Facility	- Asset VP - Asset managers - Operations managers
Driver Metrics	**Functionally specific to drive e2e business performance**	- Facility - Functions e.g. Maintenance, Operations	- Operations manager - Functional General Managers
Process Metics	**Process and procedures compliance** that impact functional performance	- Facility - Function	- Operations Managers - Functional managers

Fig. 5.24 The performance pyramid

Function	Leading KPI
Integrated activity planning	Stable plan
Production asset	Realistic required on-site date
Material management	Stock accuracy Process time
Procurement	Contract readiness
Inbound logistics	Accurate lead times

Figure 5.25 illustrates the KPIs appropriate to the different levels in the organisation and the intended audience that should receive them.

At level 1 these KPIs should be common across the industry. You only need to look into benchmarking companies to realise how unstructured this space is for the Oil and Gas industry. At levels 2 and 3, the KPIs have to be relevant in relation to the state of maturity of the functions. Thus, they should not be static but driven by the needs of that business at that particular moment in time.

A good illustration of this relates back to 2008 when safety was being driven hard in the industry. If the leading indicators at L2 and 3 had been operational at that time, the business would have focussed KPIs on personal safety, i.e. holding the handrail, using seat belts and not walking under suspended loads. In 2012, the focus changed to Process Safety and these KPIs should have been changed to reflect this new focus. Again in 2018, these KPIs would have been changed to System Patterns.

What is important for the KPIs is that they are relevant to the business, the time and environment in which it is operating. The current focus should be on CO_2 emissions, and a leading KPI could be 'Are we building sufficient gas storage and compression to stop the need for flaring?' The problem is we just have a single lagging KPI to measure this 'how much flaring has happened' without any Leading KPIs to support this.

There are three things we need to be careful about in the structure illustrated in Fig. 5.25

(a) Make sure there are no lagging indicators in level 3 and a balance of Leading and Lagging at level 2. Lagging indicators at L3 will absolve ownership of the KPI as there are too many dependencies. Lagging indicators at L3 should be treated with suspicion and challenged at all accounts. Figure 5.26 gives an example of how these KPIs could look.

(b) There is a real risk, and it has been observed that the leadership has an inflexibility towards KPI once they are onboarded. It is critical that the breadth and depth of KPI in the organisation are kept relevant and concise. This means less relevant or irrelevant KPIs should be jettisoned to make room for current relevant ones.

    If this does not happen then a proliferation of KPIs will swamp the business, which in turn will allow people to choose the ones they want and will ultimately deliver suboptimal results. Keep them tight and keep them relevant. Getting rid of a KPI does not mean it was always wrong, just that it is not right for the current moment in time.

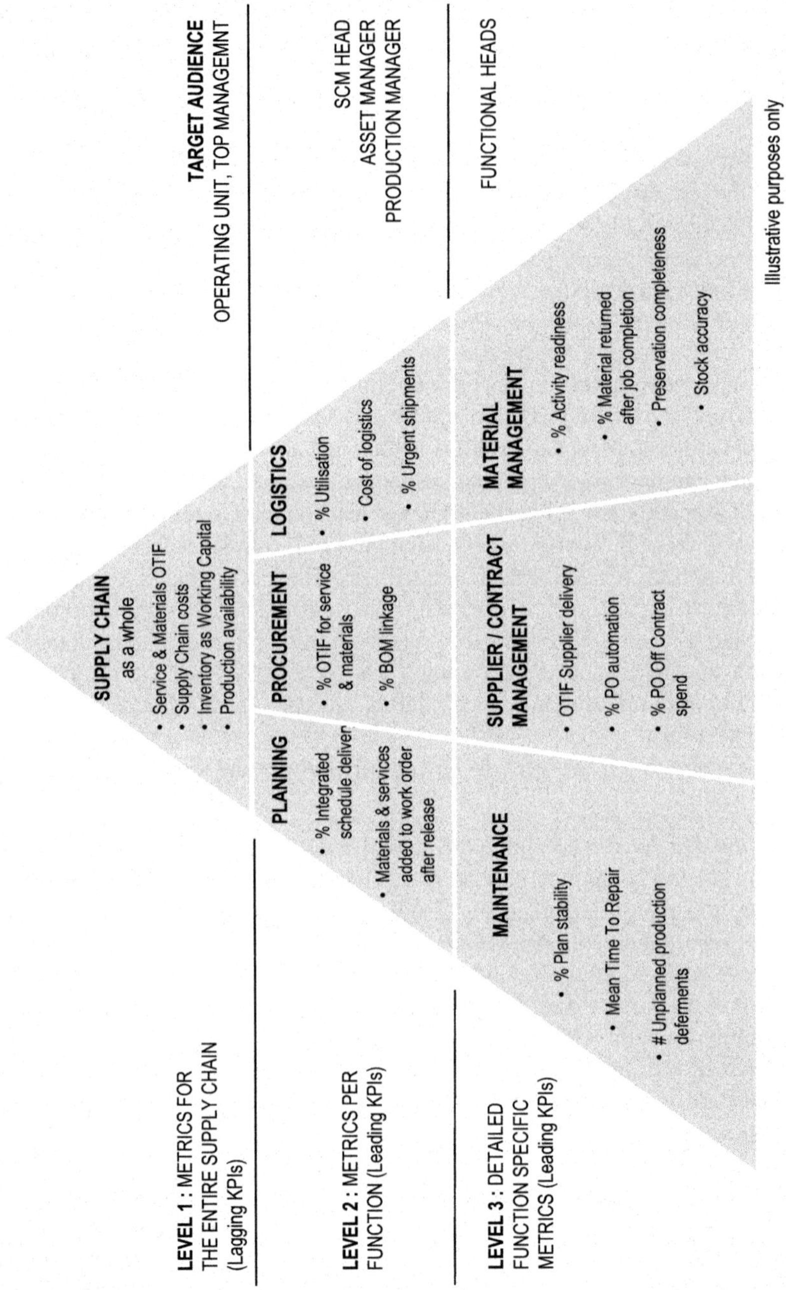

Fig. 5.25 The KPI tree of a supply chain

End to End alignment

METRIC LEVEL	PRODUCTION	OPEX	CAPEX EFFICIENCY
Business Performance Metrics	• Availability • Planned vs. actual production • Capacity utilisation	• Opex per BOE production (Planned vs. actual)	• Project costs: Actual vs. target • Time per Well • Cost per Well
Driver Metrics	• Schedule adherence • Planned vs unscheduled deferment	• Productivity (% capacity utilised) • Logistics costs • Maintenance spend • Turnaround cycle time • Labour costs	• Design standardisation and replication
Process Metics by Functions (Maintenance, Service, Procurement)	• Deferment by reason code • Planning backlog	• Maintenance plan completeness • Standby time • Inventory costs	• Plan stability • Schedule exceptions
	• OTIF performance • Inventory vs. target	• Logistics utilisation • Inventory carrying costs	• Logistics schedule compliance • OTIF performance
		• Use of standardised purchaing channels	• Material cost reduction

Fig. 5.26 Aligning the KPIs towards business delivery

End to End alignment

L1	% Material On Time	Lagging
L2	% MOT by function	Lagging
	Plan Changes	Leading
	Material master data accuracy	Leading
L3	Planning: Management Of Change Process adherence	Leading
	Asset: Realistic required on site date	Leading
	Materials Management: Stock accuracy	Leading
L4	Culture: 5S, SOP, Problem Solving, Training & Development	Neither leading or lagging but the bedrock of the organisation.

Fig. 5.27 Leading and lagging indicators

(c) Often organisations include KPIs as shown in level 4 in Fig. 5.27, however, these are not really genuine KPIs, these are enablers and not drivers. They do create the building blocks for the organisation and are an essential component in its success.

It is critical to embed the KPIs to deliver across L3 and then L2 and finally L1. Focussing on L4 KPIs is seldom beneficial. Do not fall into the trap of measuring how many people have been trained as this does nothing for the KPI of the business. The next section deals with the importance of dealing with this level.

5.1.12 5-W Versus 5-Why's

Most problem resolutions start with the 5-W—Who, What, When, Where, Why (Fig. 5.28). This is a good solid approach to get an understanding of a specific situation, what happened, why and how it happened as well as when it happened. It is a tool that gets to an answer quickly and enables a plan to be put in place. This approach is used extensively in the Oil and Gas industry, at all levels throughout the organisation. At the asset, the operators, maintenance staff and management are keen

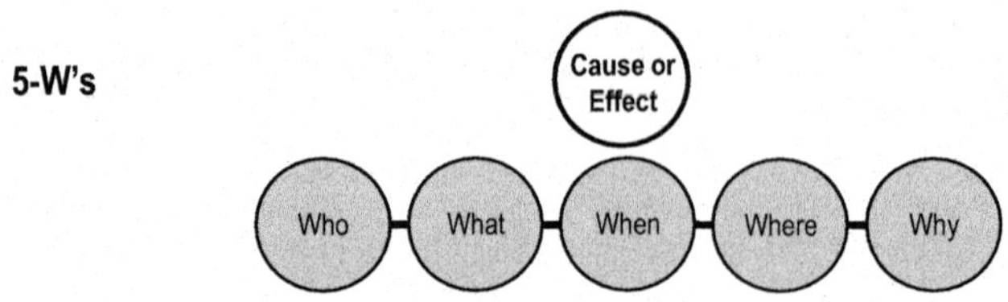

Fig. 5.28 The 5-W

to get the problem understood and resolved as quickly as possible to get production back online as quickly as possible. At the higher management levels, the problem solving has a similar nature, in part due to it always being done that way and in part being wary of the next crisis already in the making. This gets the business to an immediate technical solution, but rarely does it solve the problem in a sustainable way.

The common approach to Lean is to focus specifically on 'Why' in the 5-W, to develop this further into 5-Why's, which is specifically driven around a series of 'why' questions to identify the root cause of a problem in order to establish a relevant solution. Whereas the 5-W gets to a speedy solution, which is deployable and often resolves the issue, the 5-Why's dig much deeper into the causal reasons behind a situation and will deliver a long-term sustainable solution. A great practice is to use the 5-W as a starting point to establish the scope of the problem and then progress to 5-Why's to drive a more precise solution to the issue.

In the supply chain, however, to be successful it is not sufficient to have just a strong 5-W capability, we must also develop our 5-Why's skills (Fig. 5.29) because the majority of the challenges are not from within the functional domains but almost always across them and beyond to include external parties.

The 5-W organisation spends much of its time describing the structure of the problem rather than understanding what needs to be done about it. It attempts to answer the issue from a technical perspective only rather than a causal perspective.

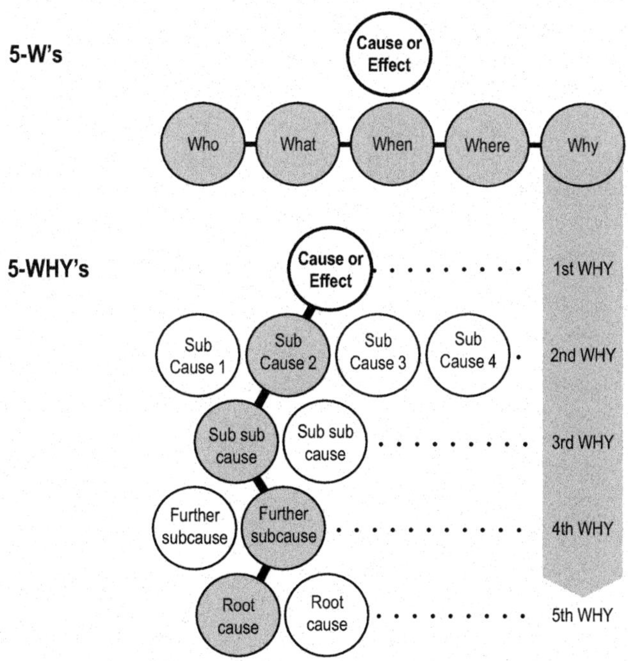

Fig. 5.29 The 5-W and the 5-Why's

An organisation focussed on 5-Why's identifies the root cause of a problem with the objective of finding a sustainable solution to it.

Can an organisation rely entirely on a 5-W expertise? Yes it can, however, the resolution will be short lived and the issue will often reoccur requiring the same problem to be solved multiple times. However, deploy the 5-Why's approach after the first incident and the problem has a much higher probability of being resolved at the root cause level preventing recurrence.

In order to achieve a successful drilling campaign, it is essential that problems encountered are solved safely and quickly. This is a classic situation where a technical problem needs an immediate solution for a successful outcome. In the Oil and Gas industry, we are experts in technical problem solving. These issues need to be solved by the experts in that field within a short period by people who may not have the luxury of time for detailed analysis. In comparison, solving the problem of ensuring the right material and resources are in place to address the issues for the same drilling campaign is an organisational problem that requires prior planning and external engagements. The 5-Why's approach delivers a continuous improvement mindset that builds the organisational problem-solving muscle.

For problem solving, we should not expect everyone to understand each other's functions in detail, however, it is important that we understand the interdependencies and impact on the rest of the value stream. We should be prepared to receive feedback and proactively jointly solve problems even when issues occur further along the value stream. It is therefore critical that we have a common language across the functions for problem solving. The most successful organisations are ones who do not waste 80% of their time trying to understand each other, instead, they spend 80% of the time solving and improving the situation.

The Oil and Gas industry is often exceptional at vertical problem solving and often receives plaudits for the work in this area, e.g. HSSE management and new drilling techniques. However, opportunity lies in solving issues across organisational interfaces and by addressing this weakness we will undoubtedly save both resources and expenditure.

Chapter 6
When Culture Meets Transformation

The definition of insanity, according to Einstein, is to keep doing the same thing over and over again but expecting different results. So would the right answer be to take the opposite approach and always try something totally different? Neither of these tactics is effective—the first one is akin to banging your head against a brick wall with invariably no noticeable change except perhaps a sore head. The second approach can have such a disruptive impact on the culture of the organisation that it can end up doing more harm than good and if it is done too often, it can appear that the leadership is clutching at straws maybe to appease shareholders rather than to secure the longevity of the business.

Reorganisations are often the straws that large corporations clutch at, an unhappy combination of doing the same thing whilst changing everything. So what is really going on? Why does this approach not work? Should businesses avoid reorganisations?

Well, the problem here is that there is no feedback loop, one which identifies why the last reorganisation did not achieve as much as it should or what external factors have changed enough to require something to be modified or changed completely. Those businesses that have a heightened sense of awareness are typically the ones who make corrective adjustments which are much more successful than those who make wholesale changes. It is not uncommon for a change in leadership to start with an immediate reorganisation, perhaps as a point to prove that this leadership will be different from the last or that the new leader wants to be seen to be their own person who is not content with inheriting the previous organisation. However, this in itself, talks more to the leadership culture than it does about organisational effectiveness. It indicates there is a lack of a cohesive leadership direction for the business and a much stronger individual competitive streak.

Often during a reorganisation, the control of the helm is given to individuals with a high potential or who are on a fast-tracked development programme with significant sponsorship. In the process, the true knowledge and experience often get side-tracked as the focus shifts to 'new' ideas and strategies that the new leader feels

S. Roy, S. Dunbar, *Improving Supply Chains in the Oil and Gas Industry*, Springer Series in Supply Chain Management 16,
https://doi.org/10.1007/978-3-030-95066-8_6

compelled to introduce. Else how is the promotion justified if you have not found things to fix and turn around in the first 90 days? Although this may appear to be a cynical view it occurs often in large organisations, indeed sometimes it is an expectation of the new leadership team. Every organisation has its own capability to successfully deal with such disruptions and come out stronger. The question we should ask ourselves is if this approach should remain a practice in an industry that must reinvent itself to remain competitive.

If the reorganisation button is hit too frequently, regardless of the leadership narrative, the teams end up going into survival mode. Fear and anxiety take root and there is no real commitment towards the business. This is no doubt the biggest indirect loss for an organisation, that is when the spirit of its community is amputated. The resulting culture is resistant to change, shy of trying new approaches and has little spirit to continuously improve.

Faced with rapid changes in the marketplace, the software companies have learned, adopted and mastered the Agile way of working. This was based on a cadence way of working with incremental progress check-in and firm commitment from Leadership to front line and it delivered against stretch targets, often exceeding them.

This type of approach was adopted by one of the North Sea Operating Unit, once on the brink of divestment turned themselves around by this culture of focussing on clear, measurable objectives, that contributed to the overall goals. A weekly follow up and culture of making small but firm progress. Teams openly shared ideas and sought help if they hit a roadblock regardless of their functional domains. So remarkable was this cultural shift that this unit became the recipient of capex investments for future growth in a few years, as opposed to a candidate ready for divestment.

If it had not been for the discovery of Penicillin by Alexander Fleming in 1928 and the subsequent further developments by the Department of Pathology at Oxford University and the biochemist Norman Heatley, we may still have been dying in hospitals from blood infections caused by cuts or scratches. Aside from the remarkable achievement of developing the first antibiotic which could be mass produced, the way it was developed was a great example of collaboration. People learned from each other, taking what was already known, making changes to it and enhancing it. Whilst Fleming discovered penicillin, it took the combined effort of five companies in total to bring it to the masses.

To draw a parallel from the two case studies, the biggest changes and remarkable progress come from a culture of openness, sharing good ideas and building upon each other's achievements to deliver what may seem an impossible task. Continuity helps on the journey as people are naturally resilient to changes and rise up to challenges if they do not have to operate in a mode of survival. This culture can hold its ground against big changes in a way that a set of reorganisations will never deliver.

We have often been told that what works in Japan may not work in the USA and what works in the USA will certainly not work in Nigeria. The challenge being that there is too big a difference in the culture. True, the communities in these countries have a different society, a different history and political setup which make them unique. However, if we shift our focus to communities in an organisation, even with the geographical diversities, it is possible to create a strong sense of purpose that transcends these cultural differences. Today in the world of social media, communities are formed across political boundaries on varied topics of interest. These communities can get a momentum that has power to influence individuals, societies and politics.

A diverse community with a common purpose can come together to address issues jointly and the role of leadership is to create an atmosphere where problems can be shared, solutions freely traded and great ideas replicated and enhanced. This requires a different cadre of leadership who do not come to the table, with readymade strategies and solutions but focus on (a) defining the targets in response to the current situation plus future trends and (b) creating an atmosphere where culture of experimentation, collaboration and rapid problem solving can thrive.

Having said this, we recognise that this might be easier to practice in large international oil companies versus the indigenous ones. Since the government is involved and material purchases are seen as national assets, there is a reluctance to deviate from old processes even if they are inefficient. We have observed paper-based processes where every decision must be signed and countersigned by multiple layers of leadership to distribute the decision across multiple stakeholders. This avoids direct ownership and persecution if something goes wrong and the consequence may even lead to a prison sentence. Such draconian outcomes surely stifle any desire for change.

In our opinion, such work cultures have no place in the current and future societies. Unable to modernise in a rapidly changing society these national industries need to invest in new ways of working, adoption of new technology that drives transparency to stay relevant in a low oil price future. As it has been said and what we have observed working across many countries, when culture is pitted against transformation, culture will eat transformation (or reorganisation) for breakfast every day.

6.1 Culture Through Organisation

The major catalysts for culture are the senior leadership themselves and they need a specific set of skills in order to be successful. They must understand their role in embedding and promoting a continuous improvement culture rather than just using the continuous improvement terms and phrases. We need more leaders who are effective coaches. A leader who dictates is not as effective as one who leverages and coaches their people. The power of the whole is greater than the sum of the individuals.

A Leader should be an ambassador of continuous improvement and does not need to be an expert practitioner. The key to coaching is helping people think for themselves, to use their own knowledge and understanding to drive a better solution. Culture is the way an organisation naturally responds to a common stimulus

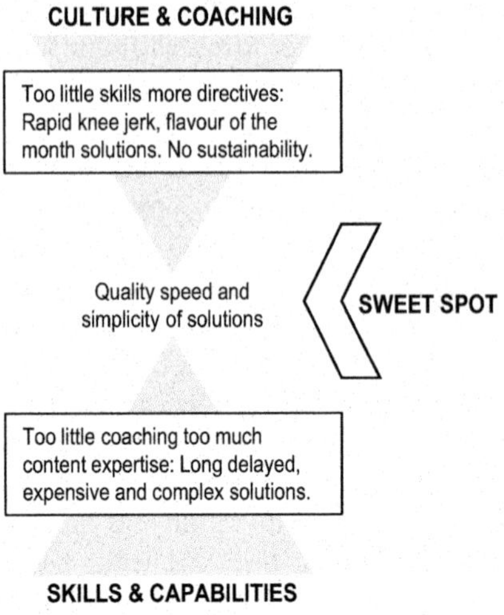

Fig. 6.1 The balance of culture and capabilities. The real task of leadership

regardless of the function, it has a common understanding of its purpose and clarity on how each individual is contributing to that purpose.

Thus, the Nobel prize winner economist Amartya Sen quotes, 'Culture is the smell of a place'. Culture is driven from the top down and is defined by the leadership by their everyday actions. The skills and capability drive the quality of the solution provided and are driven from the bottom up. These skills are manufactured and delivered in house or by recruiting externally those with the right talents. The combination of the top-down culture and coaching with the bottom-up skills and capability determines the quality, speed and relevance of the solutions created.

All organisations should also be aligned in delivering a balanced scorecard (Fig. 6.1) and although not an exact science, the sum total of all the individual targets should reflect the direction the business wants to move. If this summation has a bias towards delivering a transactional outcome, then the organisation is typically focused on delivering for survival. If it has a significant bias toward a strategic objective, then the organisation is focussed on the future and is potentially suffering losses now (e.g. a start-up enterprise). Established organisations should be somewhere in the middle, delivering now (transactional) and planning for the future (strategic). However, it is not unusual for even established companies to have a focus on annual-based targets which detracts the business and typically pushes the overall organization to the right (Fig. 6.2). Success and rewards are therefore based on the 'in-year' achievements, rather than looking forward at the growth and longevity of the business for the future.

This is even more exacerbated the higher up the organisation you progress. Sure, there are senior leaders whose main aim in life is to deliver the cash, to produce the goods and fund the business today. However, even in this situation it is critical that they have a good connection with the strategic side of the bow tie to ensure what they

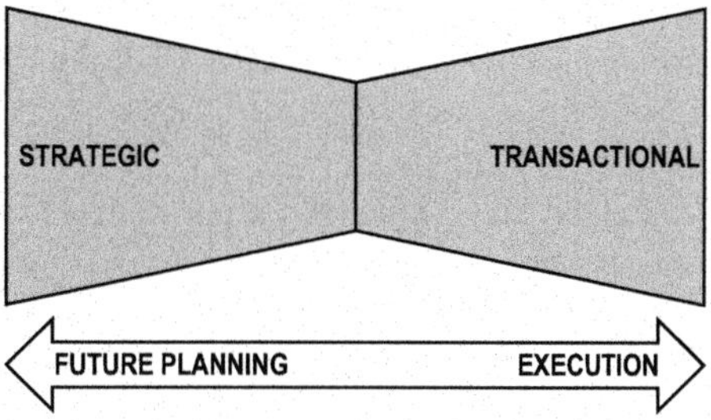

Fig. 6.2 The balance between strategy and execution

do now is in the context of future strategy and does not impair or derail the future direction.

So how does this apply to the supply chain? Well in many organisations it is seen as a cost centre, rather than what it is—the lifeblood of the organisation. It is critical that the Chief Supply Chain Officer (CSCO) role is defined and operates at the right level in the organisation although this often depends on the maturity of the supply chain function within the organisation. Embryonic organisations should be biased their focus towards the left of centre (strategy), ensuring that a credible supply chain is first of all defined and then created. As it matures, it should move towards a more central position to ensure the right balance between strategy and execution. A bias towards the right will ultimately result in a supply chain organisation that is too heavily focused on cost saving, which in turn drives poor behaviours.

The aim of the CSCO is to drive the supply chain forward, not only to set the directions, but to manage and enable more end-to-end integration. To do this the role has to increase the supply chain capability and to be able to paint the picture of the end goal along with the major steps in getting there. This should form the basis of the goals for the rest of the Supply Chain organisation and it is critical that this goal setting is done meticulously to set the tone for the rest of the organisation.

In most cases, efficiencies are driven by the *need* rather than a *strategy* to become more efficient. This 'short-termism' results in decisions being made that often drive long-term inefficiencies as well as a localised cost reduction focus which will hurt vendors and undermine the collaboration required with them. If there is no overall high-level supply chain strategy solutions are always derived at a tactical level.

6.2 Technology Shopping

Recently, we observed that in a particular business, most of the top quartile digital 'toys' had been bought and deployed without sufficient attention to how they integrated the end-to-end value stream. As a result, with a suite of best-in-breed solutions, the teams were still working with manual information gathering and Excel spreadsheets. Perhaps in the world of supply chains, the Oil and Gas industry has the most catching up to do regarding digital tools. It is not that they cannot afford this technology, after all single wells cost many millions to drill, but with a 5 What approach (defined previously) the focus has been on delivering a technical solution rather than using data to make supply chains and operations more efficient (i.e. a 5 Why approach). The use of data has been primarily in engineering development, exploration etc.

Lately, there has been a surge in adoption of digital tools. Following articles in newspapers such as The Economist, stating that Oil and Gas data is more valuable than the oil and gas itself, there has been a series of engagements between the monarchs of digital domain and the oil industry executives, who realise that unless we capitalise and make better use of our data, our business performance is at risk, and we cannot depend on oil prices alone. This is a welcome change and transition towards modernisation of rather archaic supply chains.

On the journey, the leaders need to take into consideration a few aspects that can impede the impact of technology adoption and that indeed comes back to culture. We must align the team towards what the technology is supposed to enable and why that is important. Adding technology is easy, they are plentiful in the marketplace. However, it must address a clear specific pain point where we are bleeding in the value chain. Without a clear business case and or without a follow-up on delivery, we are just delivering a hobby horse.

Any technical solution should be clearly based on user needs. It should *supplement* the current initiatives and be aligned with the overall business purpose. Developing in isolation and then expecting a broad adoption across the business often delivers a quick solution but alienates the stakeholders. This results in wasted development time and cash whilst undermining internal relationships. In an oil and gas industry where digital stock tracking (i.e. barcodes) is still a novelty, perhaps the attention should be more towards adopting industry standard solutions rather than bespoke in-house developments.

Technology itself does not normally deliver the results it must be supported by the organisation and therefore culture is critical in a successful deployment. Even with new enablers, the leaders will have to spend time coaching and encouraging the teams to adopt new ways of working. The most successful, do this by walking the talk. They will review the situation using the operational tools rather than static data snap shots in presentations. Leadership should be directed and encouraged to view the key performance indicators directly in digital tools and we should limit generating non-value-adding reports and updates. As the old saying goes, 'What interests my boss fascinates me!'

Although this is not a new concept and has been said many times before, it seems a hard lesson to learn by most organisations. In a rush to show results and deploy shiny new tools, it is often the case that poorly designed processes are digitised. Therefore, with a poor understanding of what parts of the processes are value adding, often the non-value-adding parts are digitised, rather than pruned or redesigned prior to digitisation. So what happens? You still get a poor output, just that it is produced faster and provided by an expensive digital tool! There is but a simple mantra to be adopted by all leaders—improve first and digitise second.

Finally, we must be cognizant of the inherent capacity of any organisation to absorb change. Technology deployment must be aligned with the ability of the business to keep up with it. Deploy too fast, which is the tendency, and you will lose the audience. Pace the introduction of digital tools as part of an overarching multigenerational deployment plan. Communicate often to ensure that continuity and interdependencies are always clear. This is where a good interface between the supply chain leader and the IT deployment team is critical. It must be thought of as 'business process digitisation' rather than 'digital tool deployment'.

6.3 Organisational Design to Meet Your Goals

Supply chain KPIs are much more than delivery or replenishment performance or indeed cycle time and cost reduction. We must consider a multidimensional approach to improving the overall efficiency and sustainability of the organisation.

The CSCO must champion the supply chain as the lifeblood of the organisation rather than a support to the cash engine (production). They must be capable of driving the future agenda, development and strategy rather than being defined by delivery of the current set of KPIs. The focus must be more towards the future than they are currently. If this approach is neglected it will drive exactly the same outcome in the future as there is today regardless of the organisational structure changes. Change the behaviours through expertise rather than simply changing the organisation structure.

The Oil and Gas industry should deliberately seek and attract experienced recruits at the highest level of supply chain to drive the change. These organisations need a change agent at the top who will present a very different paradigm and perspective of the purpose and design of the supply chain, that is much broader than just procurement and material supply management. Their task is to create a 'supply chain' or better still 'supply ecosystem' which reacts to changes in an agile manner where all parties involved feel listened to and part of the solution.

Recently, we observed in several large oil companies a trend of Procurement specialists being appointed into Supply Chain roles. In our view, this transition of Procurement professionals towards Supply Chain professionals is a good step forward. However, just a job title change is not sufficient, it must be supplemented with a fundamental understanding of how supply chains work and its role in the business. A good supply chain team should be a combination of strong procurement and supply chain execution experience. In the absence of this holistic approach, procurement experts will miss the operational supply chain expertise and focus on cost improvement rather than improving the entire supply chain. On the flip side, the absence of seasoned procurement experience often leads to fulfilling demands of the functions regardless of cost. It is essential that the right balance is struck during the transition to a Supply Chain organisation.

A supply chain leader needs to define the target summit and perhaps also the first base camp. The next biggest task should be to develop the skills and culture that rapidly defines the next base camp and the journey towards it. The common practice is to loosely define the destination, identify the tools to get there (projects) but completely miss the routes and skills necessary to deliver it. Sometimes the end goal cannot be achieved through a straight line or by cutting and pasting solutions from other deployments. Since the business and market are a dynamic force, it is of critical importance that the team adapts to dynamic forces while still focussed on the destination. The focus must shift from dictating the next steps to creating a focus on continuous improvement towards the end goal.

6.3.1 How Do You Continuously Improve?

There are repeatable processes in all industries, and these are the very foundation of any business operation. Recognising and making them more efficient using the simple code of Plan Do Review should become ingrained in the culture of any organisation. Often teams and leadership believe that this method stifles creativity, or this is suitable only for certain cultures and is not necessarily the mindset acceptable in societies that encourage individualism and personal growth. It is true that in this area culture makes a difference, but these sceptics miss a subtle and important distinction, repeatable tasks create standardisation, without which you can never improve. We should unleash creativity to solve all issues and obstacles that prevent an effective and error-free execution of the required standard. Variations in standards can drive up cost and increase the number of safety incidents.

There is a perception even in capital projects that every project is unique and therefore there is no attempt to apply continuous improvement, this is the domain of the manufacturing industry, isn't it? Once again, the difference is subtle but a remarkable one. If you view the project as a unique product being developed at one station, the crew and material required to produce it are constantly changing in order to build that one off unique product. But even if it is a truly unique project (which they rarely are) there are repeatable processes that should be adopted for instance handover from one crew to next, transfer of quality standards, defining the safety standards, the expectation of daily target setting and its delivery from one crew to next and so on. These are all repeatable processes even in a unique capital project.

Often the teams and organizations try to learn from the 'After Action Review' (AAR). This is like learning from a post-mortem. It will tell you the cause of death, 5 Whats, but had the 5 Whys been carried out earlier the death could have been prevented through early detection and elimination. This is exactly what a culture of Plan Do Improve embeds in an organization. AAR is not important by itself but from the lessons we learn from it and what we do with them.

A humble 'learning mindset' is at the core of everything. Somewhere on our journey we stop learning and the challenge for any leader is to rekindle that spark in every team member.

Chapter 7
Getting Started

Another version of Einstein's definition of insanity, attributed to Henry Ford is that 'if you always do what you have always done you will always get what you've always got'. The British coxed 8's rowing team used this wisdom to begin their training for their preparation for the 2000 Olympic Games in Sydney. They translated this into a question they asked before any training session or decision taken 'will it make the boat go faster?' If it moved them towards their goal, then they did it, if it did not then they did not do it. This approach even extended to them attending the opening ceremony, they asked themselves would attending this event make the boat go faster? What they decided was it would interrupt their training; it would interrupt their eating plan; it would interrupt their sleep. Consequently, they chose to watch the opening ceremony on the television in the Olympic village like the rest of the world. No doubt they got some significant negative press for doing this, but on 24th September 2000 at 10:30 am, they started a race in which they were not the favourites to win because they were being judged on previous performances of the British team in the Olympics. But the win they did and the hard work they put in to change the way they approached their training resulted in them beating Australia in the final by almost a second.

Any organisation needs to look carefully at its approach and response to the future. Will the actions being taken truly make their own boat go faster or is it simply a repeat of what has been done in the past? From a supply chain perspective, in a difficult market, will negotiating harder with your suppliers or cutting jobs really make the business more profitable for now and the future or will it simply pacify today's need but create a problem for tomorrow? Is it good enough to simply appease the investors?

It is crucial then that any supply chain organisation secures acknowledgement of the importance it has in the business and gets recognised as the lifeblood for delivery. It must invest time and effort in strategically developing itself during the good times when it will contribute to the business profitability and is resilient during the bad times to ensure endurance.

S. Roy, S. Dunbar, *Improving Supply Chains in the Oil and Gas Industry*, Springer Series in Supply Chain Management 16,
https://doi.org/10.1007/978-3-030-95066-8_7

It is essential that the supply chain develops its own balanced scorecard to ensure that it delivers across the various aspects rather than simply relying on 'the way it has always been'. These scorecards must be assessed to make sure they align with the goals of the business, and they have the right balance between delivering now and improving for the future.

If you recognise some, maybe all, of the issues raised in this book in your organisation, you might identify with some or all of the 12 modules that can benefit your organisation. You will no doubt have other areas where you need to focus on, but what is critical is that you ensure you follow the steps below.

7.1 Define Where You Want to Be

Define where you want to be (North Star) as the umbrella for a consolidated journey. This will help to visualise the future desired supply chain both at an organisational and an individual level. This will give a purpose and a view of the 'promised land'. Senior leaders need to be fully conversant with what this looks like and how it benefits the industry as much as how it benefits the organisation since individuals are key to enabling the transformation. Transformation does not happen because of a plan but because those involved buy into that plan. Invest more energy into the 'buy in' rather than delivering a perfect plan.

Figure 7.1 compares the traditional procurement approach to supply chain, where cost is central to the decision-making. However, do not be seduced by trying to deliver the cheapest option. Do not let the procurement mindset of 'lowest cost' determine your supply chain strategy, but consider: resilience, agility, consistency and quality in addition to cost.

7.2 Establish Where You Are

It is important to be honest with yourself as an organisation of where you actually are at present. There is a tendency for people to become defensive, it was not my fault, I did the best I could etc. So, focus on the data. Remove the outliers and look at the variability of what remains. Again, do not be distracted by outliers, our experience has shown that 80% of energy is spent around outliers where leaders think that attention here will help the organisation the most. However, this is also a totally wrong assumption, as Fig. 7.2 shows, the focus should be on compressing the variability around the median performance, there will always be outliers and the resolution of these will not help the majority.

Data-driven decisions for improvement are critical for success. This requires a basic understanding of statistics and the visualisation of data, which unfortunately is an essential component that is missing in many organisations.

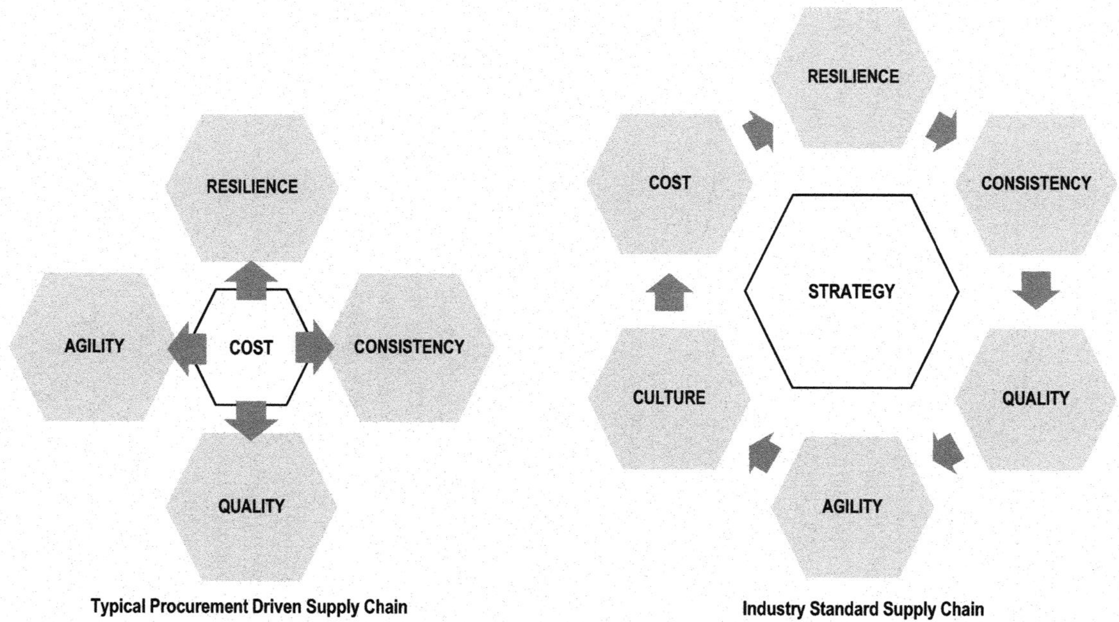

Fig. 7.1 The mindset of procurement driven supply chains vs. industry standards and requirements

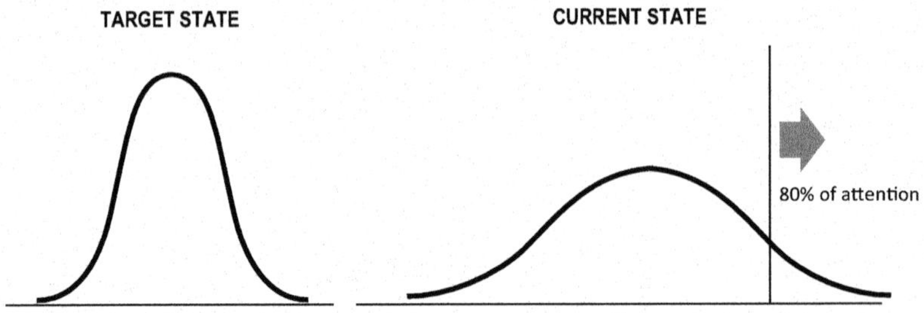

Fig. 7.2 Variations can distract the entire leadership

It can be seen that many organisations prefer to listen to and act on a good story regardless of whether it is backed up by fact or not. The story is the important part, where those who are good orators are more successful. If this is not counterbalanced by data-driven decisions, the strategy can often be flawed. The 80% attention to outliers drives a business to constantly firefight which means there is no time to look at continuous improvement and therefore no advancements made to improve the core of the supply chain performance. There will ALWAYS be outliers.

> Do not focus all your attention on outliers, focus mainly on reducing the variability around the median.

The median is a woefully badly understood statistical concept, which many businesses do not recognise. The average is almost always the statistic of choice but this covers a multitude of sins and often drives the outliers to be the target of attention. The median gives much more visibility to the health of the supply chain process rather than the average which is skewed too much by the extreme outliers.

Additionally, businesses also consider their performance data to be a typical normal distribution, equally distributed on both sides of the average. If this were the case, then average and median would be very close but in reality, the supply chain performance curves are very rarely normally distributed and are usually significantly skewed (see Fig. 7.3). In this situation, the average and median are distinctly apart.

Fig. 7.3 Focusing on Outliers

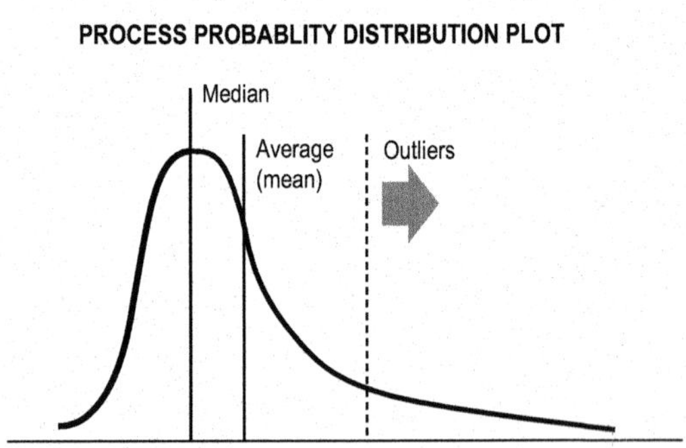

7.3 Identify What You Need to Fix

Whilst there are numerous ways of undertaking a gap analysis, one we have found extremely useful is the value stream analysis. This works on multiple levels.

1. The first level is to walk the process from end to end, requiring a documented version of what the process should be.
2. The second level would be the immediate debate on whether or not this is what is actually happening. Some corrections may become apparent even at this early stage and deliver small quick wins.
3. At the third level, you would have the understanding of the interfaces between functions and how data and information are moving from silo to silo, showing actual vs. perceived.
4. The fourth level would highlight the difference between value-added and the non-value-added activities.
5. Progressing to the fifth level will allow the functions up and down the value chain to understand the impact of their behaviours on each other.
6. The final level will deliver the recognition and mitigation of actions that usually result due to lack of trust in the value chain (order too much, order too early, keep squirrel stores active, set unnecessarily high replenishment levels etc.).

   As we know these actions create a series of bullwhips, which instead of the traditional bullwhip where one mistake at the beginning gets amplified at the end, this phenomenon has a series of mistakes (or counter actions) which actually change the outcome completely, for instance resulting in 27 football pitches of containers of unnecessary inventory!

7.4 Choose the Best Starting Point

It is important to choose your starting point very carefully. Businesses often create a 4-box matrix, with impact plotted against effort (or cost) to establish the big easy wins. The temptation is to constantly focus on these low effort improvements or quick wins. In turn, they often become all-consuming and absorb significant amounts of time and effort. These activities that drive quick wins, especially those around the biggest pain point, are a great place to start but they should be done with little (or no) senior leadership involvement, if they are simple fixes then just do it!

It is important to tackle some of those improvements that are truly transformational or else are forever consigned to the 'too difficult' or 'we'll get to those later' pile. These improvements need to be treated differently from the easy low hanging fruit ones. As mentioned earlier, not only do they need to be data driven but they must also be heavily sponsored by senior leaders and be communicated to all those whose involvement is needed to make it a success.

> Don't waste sponsorship time on simple fixes, focus it on transformational activities.

These transformational changes must take the business towards the North Star, if they do not, then either they are not the right improvements or just as possible, the north star is wrong and needs modification. It is also important to recognise that in many cases the changes to be implemented have an inbuilt sequence (i.e. activity A must happen before B and C can be delivered). Do not be under the misapprehension that everything can be done at once—to climb Everest you must pass through a series of camps, each with their own set of challenges. The leadership must recognise that in order to get to the top of Everest, the organisation must transit through these camps before achieving the desired goal.

Multi-year transformation is important (Fig. 7.4), do not fall into the trap of acceleration simply to look good, it is essential that the whole organisation goes on the journey. Go too fast and you leave critical people (especially some senior managers) behind, and they end up becoming opposed to the change rather than curious about it. Small wins are needed to prove the journey is worthwhile and capable of delivering results.

The end goal (North Star) needs to be firmly in mind through the whole transition in order to keep driving towards it. Each change will deliver benefits in their own right but the benefit of the whole is much greater than the sum of the components. We have seen that this can be difficult in organisations where people are moved roles every 3–4 years since the transformation will often last beyond the assignment of the individuals. The way to overcome this is to embed the supply chain transformation in the corporate 5+ year strategy to ensure longevity beyond the individual assignment lengths. To achieve this, an appropriate approach would be to use the same as that used in major projects.

Although tempting, it is important not to start the journey of transformation with a massive reorganisation. Instead, use the journey to define what the future organisational structure should be and have an equivalent multigenerational

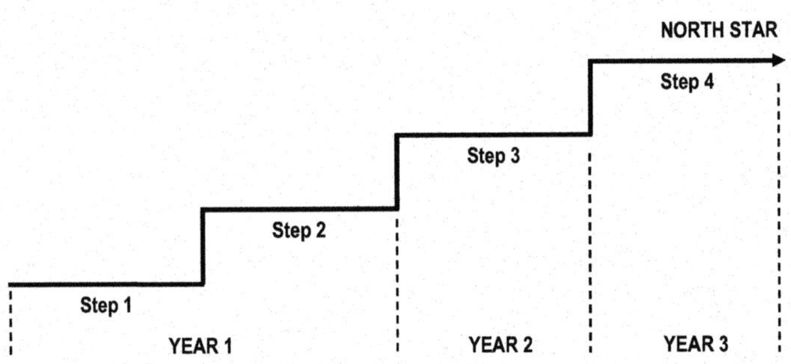

Fig. 7.4 A staged approach to transformation

organisational change plan to move the organisation towards the end goal. Rarely does a single reorganisation achieve what it was designed for or survive any length of time. It also destabilizes the organisation and undermines performance.

It is critical that the HR changes are in response to the process changes, HR changes must never be the driving factor. Use the continuous improvement approach to your organisation, change relevant areas at the right time, trying to implement a single reorganisation does NOT fit with a multi-generational project plan *MGPP* and will often derail the whole intent of the change programme. This is often the mistake made by large organisations.

> It is critical that the organisational changes are delivered in response to process changes—they must not be the driving factor.

7.5 Public Declaration of Intent

In order to deliver change in any organisation, there needs to be an alignment on the direction of travel and a commitment from the whole organisation to move in this direction. The galvanising of commitment be left to the traditional method of briefing senior leaders and expecting them to cascade to the rest of the organisation. Invariably this approach has mixed results, some leaders do it well, some not so well and some not at all. Ultimately the message at the lower levels is at best inconsistent and at worst non-existent.

In order to get the right message across one way that has been observed is to set aside specific time to brief the entire organisation. This ensures that everyone hears the same message and has the opportunity to seek clarification and better understanding from the horse's mouth as it were. It also provides the leadership with the opportunity to publicly own specific parts of the overall strategy and therefore shows a public demonstration of commitment and unity to the strategy.

Undoubtedly there are other ways of getting the message to the masses, however, expecting 'passive' communication to drive 'proactive' participation is highly unlikely to be successful. In very mature organisations, the ability to use Hoshin Kanri methodology allows a very rapid cascading of tactical and mid-term goals. However, not only does the organisation need to be skilled in using this technique, the technique itself is limited to very specific tasks and targets. From a strategy perspective, where the goal is distant and the intermediate steps are unclear, Hoshin should not replace a face-to-face type of engagement where concepts are presented, questioned and developed as part of the communication process. By engaging with the masses in this way, the level of ownership and participation increases significantly and therefore the strategy has a much greater chance of achieving the intended goal.

Needless to say, it is also important for the key elements of this strategy to be made visible and accessible to the shareholders and, where appropriate, to the market in general. The intent of the strategy should not be a secret, a public announcement makes clear the direction in which the business is aiming for, 'to be the biggest in the sulphur market', 'have the best conversion rate of prospective customers' etc.

It is important though to keep in mind the principles stated by Michael E Porter where he describes three main principles that a strategy should contain:

- A clear perspective of where the business wants to go (e.g. *a deep or a broad or a specific customer base*).
- Get the scope right, especially making the decision on what is not going to be part of the strategy.
- Ensuring it is a good fit with the activities of the business.

In 2021, many of the International Oil Companies made clear their strategy for the future of being carbon neutral, for example Shell declared that by 2035, they would be carbon neutral and that by 2050, the whole Shell supply base would be carbon neutral. This public declaration means very specific decisions will need to be taken in the medium and short term to ensure alignment with this end goal and through specific remuneration targets the whole organisation will be redirected to achieve the desired result.

> The strategy needs to be developed, declared and disseminated to be successful. Having a strategy hidden in the bottom drawer, is not having a strategy at all.

Printed by Printforce, United Kingdom